SCOTT FORESMAN · ADDISON WESLEY

Mathematics

Grade 3

Problem Solving Masters/Workbook

PEARSON

Scott Foresman

Editorial Offices: Glenview, Illinois • Parsippany, New Jersey • New York, New York

Sales Offices: Parsippany, New Jersey • Duluth, Georgia • Glenview, Illinois
Coppell, Texas • Ontario, California • Mesa, Arizona

ISBN 0-328-04961-1

2 3 4 5 6 7 8 9 10 V084 09 08 07 06 05 04 03

Ways to Use Numbers

Birdhouses Carmen and her mother are building birdhouses. First, they measured 6 ft of wood. Second, they cut the wood. Third, they nailed the pieces of wood together. Carmen and her mother made three birdhouses.

1. What ordinal numbers are in the story about building birdhouses?

   _____

2. What number is used as a measurement in the story?

   _____

3. What number is used as a count in the story?

   _____

Lunch Time Four students were in line in the lunch room. Martha was not first or fourth. Cory was ahead of Martha but behind Ricci. Greg was behind Martha.

4. What ordinal numbers are mentioned in the lunch time story?

   _____

5. Write the order of the students in line from first to fourth.

   _____

6. **Writing in Math** Write a sentence about a time you used a number to measure.

   _____

   _____

   _____

Numbers in the Hundreds

Art Museum Jefferson Elementary students took a field trip to the art museum. At the museum, there are paintings and pencil drawings.

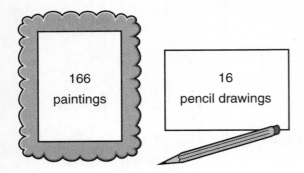

166 paintings

16 pencil drawings

1. What digit is in the ones place of both of these numbers? _____

2. Both of the numbers contain the digits 1 and 6. Are the numbers equal? Explain.

_____

Endangered Species The table below shows the number of endangered plants and animals in 2001.

Endangered Species in 2001	
Plants	737
Animals	507

3. What is the word form for the number of endangered animals? _____

4. What digit is in the hundreds place of the number of endangered plants? _____

5. **Writing in Math** Explain how you know that the number of endangered plants is different from the number of endangered animals.

_____

_____

Place-Value Patterns

Bones Sarah's class is studying bones. They have learned that there is a total of 206 bones in the adult human body. There are 64 bones in the arms and hands. There are 62 bones in the legs and feet.

1. Represent the number of bones in the arms and hands by drawing tens and ones blocks.

2. Is it possible to represent the number of bones in the human body using only hundreds blocks and tens blocks?

_____

_____

Getting to School Students at Hickory Elementary were asked how they get to school.

- 300 take the bus

- 212 walk

- 43 ride their bikes

3. Which of the numbers in the problem can be represented using only the hundreds blocks? _____

4. David said that the number of students who walked each day was equal to 212 tens. Is he correct? Explain.

_____

5. **Writing in Math** Explain how you could rename 490 using only tens.

_____

Numbers in the Thousands

Backpacks A store ordered one thousand, four hundred ninety-seven backpacks to sell at their back-to-school sale.

1. Write the number of backpacks in standard form. _____

2. Jeremy represented the number of backpacks as shown. Is his work correct? Explain.

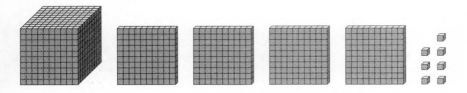

_____

3. The store manager wants to display 1,000 backpacks on shelves. Each shelf holds 100 backpacks. How many shelves will the store manager need?

_____

4. Last year, the store sold a total of 1,421 pencils. Hannah said the store sold more than 14 hundred pencils. Is she correct? Explain.

_____

_____

5. **Writing in Math** What is the least possible number you can write with a 1 in the thousands place? How can you be sure your answer is correct?

_____

_____

_____

Greater Numbers

State	Population
Alaska	634,892
Montana	904,433
North Dakota	634,448
Vermont	613,090

1. Write the population of Vermont in expanded form.

_____

2. Which states have a population with a 4 in the thousands place?

_____

3. What is the value of the digit 8 in the
population of Alaska?   _____

Ocean	Depth
Pacific Ocean	15,215 ft
Atlantic Ocean	12,881 ft
Indian Ocean	13,002 ft

4. Which ocean has a depth with the same digit in the ten-thousands place
and in the ones place?

_____

5. Write the depth of the Indian Ocean in expanded form.

_____

6. **Writing in Math** Give the value of the 2 in each ocean's
depth. Which value is the greatest?

_____

Name_____

Read and Understand

Moving Vans Grayson Moving Company has 5 moving vans at each of its locations. The company has 3 locations. How many vans does the company have?

[**Read and Understand**]

Step 1: What do you know?

1. Tell the problem in your own words.

_____

_____

2. Identify key facts and details.

_____

Step 2: What are you trying to find?

3. Tell what the question is asking.

_____

4. Show the main idea.

_____

5. Solve the problem. Write the answer in a complete sentence.

_____

6. **Pizza Party** Penelope and her friends are having a pizza party. They have 4 small pizzas. Penelope cuts 2 of the pizzas into 4 pieces each and 2 pizzas into 6 pieces each. How many pieces of pizza are there?

_____

Comparing Numbers

Middletown Use the chart below for Exercises 1–3.

Facts About Middletown
Number of people 5,867
Students in grade school 1,010
Students in high school 732
Number of houses 2,100
Books in the library 8,463

1. Compare the number of people in Middletown to the number of books in their library. Use $<$, $>$, or $=$.

   number of people _____ number of books

2. Compare the number of students in grade school to the number of students in high school.

   number of students in grade school _____ number of students in high school

3. Write a sentence to compare the number of houses to the number of students in grade school. Use the words *greater than* or *less than*.

   _____

   _____

4. **Writing in Math** Which is greater, thirteen hundred or one thousand, two hundred? Explain how you solved this problem.

   _____

   _____

   _____

   _____

Ordering Numbers

Penny Count Mr. Smith's third-grade class collected pennies in a jar. After 3 months, the students guessed the number of pennies in the jar. After they had guessed, Mr. Smith and the students counted the pennies and wrote 1,365 on a sign.

1. Five of the guesses were 999; 1,500; 1,250; and 1,025. Write these numbers from least to greatest.

   _____

2. Of the four guesses listed in Exercise 1, which were less than the actual number of pennies?

   _____

3. Write two numbers greater than 1,200 but less than the number of pennies in the jar.

   _____

Great Lakes The Great Lakes are in the Midwest of the United States and in Canada. They are the largest lakes in the world.

Lake	Depth (in feet)
Superior	483
Michigan	279
Huron	195
Erie	62
Ontario	283

4. Write the names of all five lakes in order of their depths from least to greatest.

   _____

5. **Writing in Math** If two numbers have different numbers of digits, which one is greater? Explain how you know.

   _____

   _____

Number Patterns

Census A census is a count of all of the people in a country. The United States takes a census once every 10 years.

1. The first United States census was taken in the year 1790. Name the years that the next four censuses were taken.

   _____

   _____

2. The United States took a census in the year 2000. Name the years that the four previous censuses were taken.

   _____

   _____

Leap Year Once every 4 years, an extra day is added to the calendar. This helps the seasons match up with our calendars. When it is a leap year, there is a 29th day in February.

3. There was a leap year in 1968. Continue this pattern.

   1968, 1972, 1976, _____, _____, _____

4. There was a leap year in the year 2000. Name the years that the four previous leap years occurred.

   _____

   _____

5. **Writing in Math** What are the next three numbers in the pattern? 33, 30, 27, 24, _____, _____, _____ What is the number before 33? Explain how you know.

   _____

   _____

   _____

Rounding Numbers

School Spirit In September, several events took place at Southside School: 155 people went to the band concert, 247 people went to the softball game, and 321 people went to the art show.

1. Round the number of people that attended each event to the nearest ten.

_____

2. Which event had about 100 people more than the band concert?

_____

Car Show José attended a car show to see many types of antique cars. He saw 239 cars at the show. Gina arrived at the car show later and saw only 101 cars.

3. Round the number of cars José saw to the nearest hundred.

_____

4. Round the number of cars José saw to the nearest ten.

_____

5. Round the number of cars Gina saw to the nearest hundred.

_____

6. **Writing in Math** Write a 4-digit number that rounds to 1,000 when rounded to the nearest hundred. Explain how you got your answer.

_____

_____

PROBLEM-SOLVING SKILL

Plan and Solve

Errands Tyreece and his father went to four places on Saturday morning. They went to the grocery store last. They went to the laundromat after they went to the hardware store. They went to the post office first. In what order did Tyreece and his father visit the four places?

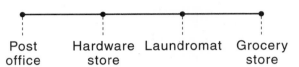

Post   Hardware   Laundromat   Grocery
office   store   store

┌──────────────────────────┐
│ **Plan and Solve**   │
└──────────────────────────┘

Step 1: Choose a strategy.

1. What strategy was used to solve the problem?

_____

Step 2: Stuck? Don't give up. Retrace your own steps.

2. What is something you can do if you get stuck?

_____

_____

Step 3: Answer the question in the problem.

3. In what order did Tyreece and his father go to the four places?

_____

_____

4. **Clown Wigs** A clown wants to choose a wig. He has a choice of 3 colors: purple, orange, or green. Each color comes in short or long hair. How many possible wig choices are there?

_____

Name_____

Counting Money

School Lunch There are two choices for lunch at Lincoln Elementary School. Lunch A costs $3.50 and Lunch B costs $3.35.

1. What bills and coins could be used to pay for Lunch A?

_____

2. What bills and coins could be used to pay for Lunch B?

_____

Pet Supplies Molly needs to buy some supplies for her new puppy. At the pet store, she will buy some of the things she needs.

3. What bills and coins could Molly use to pay for the dog food?

_____

4. Molly has 6 quarters, 2 dimes, and a nickel. Does she have enough to buy the dog bone? Explain.

_____

_____

5. **Writing in Math** Tell what coins you could use to make $0.75 in three different ways.

_____

_____

_____

Making Change

Bookstore For 1–3 use the chart below. List the coins and bills used to make change. Then write the change in dollars and cents.

Bookstore Prices	
Paperback books	$4.75
Hardcover books	$8.89
Magazines	$2.58

1. Lauren bought a magazine. She paid with three $1.00 bills.

   _____

   _____

2. Theresa bought a hardcover book. She paid with a $10.00 bill.

   _____

   _____

3. Maria bought a paperback book. She paid with a $20.00 bill.

   _____

   _____

4. **Writing in Math** John went to the garden store and bought a shovel that cost $12.62. He paid with a $10.00 bill and three $1.00 bills. Give two ways to make the change. Which used the fewest coins?

   _____

   _____

   _____

PROBLEM-SOLVING SKILL

Look Back and Check

Leaf Collections Two students have leaf collections. Frederick has 26 leaves. Yumi has 11 more leaves than Frederick. How many leaves does Yumi have?

Conchita solved the problem as shown.

26	11
37	

$$\begin{array}{r} 26 \\ + 11 \\ \hline 37 \end{array}$$

Step 1: Check your answer.

1. Was the correct question answered? Explain.

_____

_____

Step 2: Check your work.

2. Is the work shown correct? Explain.

_____

3. Did Conchita use the right operation? Explain.

_____

School Store The school store sells school supplies. A pencil costs $0.35. A ruler sells for a dime more than a pencil. A pen costs 2 quarters. How much more does a pen cost than a ruler?

Drew solved the problem as shown.

4. Was the correct question answered? Explain.

_____

_____

cost of ruler:
   $0.35 − $0.10 = $0.25

cost of pen:
   $0.25 + $0.25 = $0.50

difference in cost:
   $0.50 − $0.25 = $0.25

5. Was Drew's final answer correct? Explain.

_____

Problem-Solving Applications

Stephanie bought a new shirt that cost $23.36. She gave the clerk $24.00. Her change was 10 coins. Which coins did she receive?

Read and Understand

1. How much did the shirt cost? _____

2. How much did Stephanie give the clerk? _____

3. What are you trying to find?

_____

_____

Plan and Solve

4. What strategy will you use?

_____

5. Solve the problem and write your answer in a complete sentence.

_____

Look Back and Check

6. Explain how you can check your answer.

_____

_____

Solve Another Problem

7. Tom collected shells at the beach. He collected 33 large shells and 44 small shells. He decided to put 5 of the large shells and 7 of the small shells back on the beach. How many shells did he keep? _____

Name _____

Addition Properties

Miniature Golf Jackson and Rebecca are playing miniature golf. In miniature golf, a person's score is the number of times he or she hits the ball per hole. Each hit on the ball is called a stroke.

1. Jackson wants to find his score after playing 3 holes. On the first hole, he had 2 strokes. He had 6 strokes on the second hole and 2 strokes on the third hole. How many strokes does Jackson have altogether for 3 holes?

   _____

2. Rebecca had 3 strokes on each of the first 3 holes. Then she had 2 strokes on the fourth hole. What is Rebecca's score after playing 4 holes?

   _____

Bonnie's Stamps	
Picture	**Number of Stamps**
Flag	6
Mountain	9
Flower	5

3. How many stamps does Bonnie have altogether?

   _____

4. How many flag and flower stamps does Bonnie have?

   _____

5. **Writing in Math** If you know that $6 + 0 = 6$, how do you know that $0 + 6 = 6$? Explain.

   _____

   _____

   _____

16   Use with Lesson 2-1.

© Pearson Education, Inc. 3

Relating Addition and Subtraction

1. Hanna found 9 seashells and 2 starfish at the beach. Write a fact family to show what Hanna found on the beach.

_____

_____

Reading Colleen read 7 pages of her book in the morning and 8 pages in the afternoon.

2. Write an addition fact to find the total number of pages Colleen read.

_____

3. Write a subtraction fact to check the addition fact you used to solve Exercise 2.

_____

Place Cards Macy made 7 place cards for her party. She needs a total of 18 place cards.

4. Write a subtraction fact to find how many more place cards Macy needs to make.

_____

5. Write an addition fact to check the subtraction fact you used to solve Exercise 4.

_____

6. Writing in Math Write the rest of the fact family for $6 + 3 = 9$.

_____

Find a Rule

1. Heather put 14 in her table and got out 6. Then she put in 9 and got out 1. What rule was she using? _____

2. The rule for Austin's table is add 12. What number should Austin put in to get out 15? _____

3. The rule for Benji's table is subtract 7. What number should Benji put in to get out 2? _____

John's Garden John planted his flower boxes in an In and Out pattern.

In	✽ ✽ ✽	✽	✽ ✽		✽✽✽✽✽✽✽
Out	✽ ✽ ✽ ✽ ✽	✽ ✽ ✽	✽ ✽ ✽ ✽	✽✽✽✽✽✽	

4. Write the rule for John's In and Out pattern. _____

5. Use the rule to finish drawing the flowers in John's flower boxes.

6. Writing in Math Write your own rule for a table. Then write a complete sentence telling what number would come out if you put in 20.

_____

_____

_____

PROBLEM-SOLVING STRATEGY

Write a Number Sentence

Baseball Simon bought a baseball for $4, a bat for $12, and a cap for $3. How much money did he spend altogether?

Read and Understand

1. How much did the baseball cost? _____

2. How much did the bat cost? _____

3. How much did the cap cost? _____

4. What are you trying to find?

_____

Plan and Solve

5. Which operation will you use? _____

6. Write a number sentence. _____

7. Solve the number sentence. _____

8. Write the answer in a complete sentence.

_____

Look Back and Check

9. Explain how you can check your answer.

_____

Solve Another Problem

10. The length of Naoko's bedroom is 8 ft shorter than the length of the living room. If the living room is 21 ft long, what is the length of Naoko's bedroom? _____

Mental Math: Break Apart Numbers   PS 2-5

America's Garbage Each year Americans throw away millions of pounds of garbage. The table shows what type of garbage might be in 100 lb of garbage.

100 Pounds of Garbage in the United States	
Paper products	36 lb
Yard waste	20 lb
Food waste	9 lb
Metal	9 lb
Glass	8 lb
Plastic	7 lb
Other waste	11 lb

1. Of the 100 lb of garbage, how many pounds are paper products and yard waste? _____

2. How much does the glass and metal garbage weigh? _____

3. How much does the plastic, glass, metal, and paper products garbage weigh? _____

4. Explain how you could use mental math to figure out the combined weight of all of the garbage listed on the table.

_____

_____

_____

5. **Writing in Math** Explain how to solve 28 + 13 using mental math.

_____

_____

_____

Mental Math: Using Tens to Add

1. How many feet of space would you need for a 16 ft long saltwater crocodile to sit before a 27 ft long anaconda? _____

2. An elephant can run at a speed of 25 mi per hour. A wild turkey can travel 15 mi per hour. If the two animals started at the same point and ran in opposite directions for one hour, how many miles apart would they be? _____

Fliers Odie handed out fliers advertising the school fair. He kept track of the number of fliers he handed out during the week.

Number of Fliers
Monday—37
Tuesday—61
Wednesday—49
Thursday—26
Friday—38

3. How many fliers did Odie hand out on Wednesday and Thursday? _____

4. How many fliers did Odie hand out on Monday, Thursday, and Friday? _____

5. Odie handed out 64 fliers over the course of two days. Which two days were they?

_____

6. **Writing in Math** Use Odie's table to write your own problem that can be solved using mental math. Write the answer to your problem in a complete sentence.

_____

_____

_____

_____

Estimating Sums

Cars Passing Sanchez lives on a busy street. One morning he counted 246 cars that went by his apartment building in 1 hour. That afternoon he counted 187 cars that went by in 1 hour.

1. Estimate to the nearest hundred the number of cars that went by the apartment building during the 2 hours Sanchez was counting.

_____

2. Estimate to the nearest ten the number of cars that went by the apartment building.

_____

Animal Species Many different animals live on Earth. The chart shows the number of species of some animals.

Animal Species

Animal Group	Number of Species
Birds of prey	307
Parrots	353
Sharks	330
Whales and dolphins	83

3. Estimate the number of species of birds on the chart to the nearest hundred.

_____

4. Estimate the number of species of sharks, whales, and dolphins to the nearest hundred.

_____

5. **Writing in Math** Use the Animal Species chart to write your own problem using estimation. Write the answer in a complete sentence.

_____

_____

Overestimates and Underestimates

Sports Day Pine Wood School is having an all-sports day. Any student can gather members to form teams for the sporting events. A list of the events and the number of players needed is posted on the gymnasium door.

All-Sports Day

Sport	Number of Players
Field hockey	11
Australian football	18
Rugby	15
Soccer	11
Volleyball	6

1. Frank wants to enter the soccer and field hockey events. He estimates he will need 20 people to form the 2 teams. Will that be enough? Explain.

   _____

   _____

2. Sheila plans to form teams for Australian football and rugby. Estimate the number of players she will need to find.

   _____

3. Payton found 30 people for teams. Estimate to find if that is enough for one Australian football team and one volleyball team.

   _____

4. **Writing in Math** Use the All-Sports Day chart above and explain how you could estimate the number of students needed to form one of each team.

   _____

   _____

Mental Math: Using Tens to Subtract

The table shows how fast some animals can run.

Speeds of Animals

Animal	Speed (miles per hour)
Cheetah	65
Squirrel	12
Giraffe	32
Coyote	43
Rabbit	35
Wild turkey	15

1. How much faster is a giraffe than a squirrel?

   _____

2. How much slower is a rabbit than a coyote?

   _____

3. The difference in speed between a rabbit and another
   animal is 20 mi per hour. What is the other animal? _____

4. What is the difference in speed between the fastest
   and slowest animal on the chart? _____

5. **Writing in Math** Explain how you would use mental math
   to solve 43 − 18.

   _____

   _____

   _____

Mental Math: Counting On to Subtract

1. Polly has made 16 posters for back-to-school night. She needs 32 posters altogether. How many more does she need to make?

   _____

2. Austin is only allowed to watch 45 min of television each day. One afternoon, he watched 36 min of television. How many more minutes of television is Austin allowed to watch for the rest of the day?

   _____

3. Manuel plans to read a total of 50 pages of his book on Monday and Tuesday. He read 29 pages on Monday. How many more pages does he need to read on Tuesday?

   _____

4. To solve $84 - 43$, Davis thought of $43 + 7 = 50$. Explain what Davis should do to finish solving the problem.

   _____

   _____

   _____

5. Write two number sentences with a difference of 17.

   _____

6. Write two number sentences with a difference of 33.

   _____

7. **Writing in Math** Explain how you would count on to find $62 - 39$.

   _____

   _____

   _____

Estimating Differences

Highest Roller Coasters

Location	Height (ft)
Valencia, California	415
Gold Coast, Australia	380
Mie, Japan	318
Sandusky, Ohio	310
Yamanashi, Japan	259

1. About how much higher is the roller coaster in California than the roller coaster in Ohio?

_____

2. About how much is the difference between the heights of the two roller coasters in Japan?

_____

3. About how much is the difference between the height of the roller coaster in Australia and the height of the roller coaster with the least height?

_____

4. Micah's family spent a day at the amusement park. It took them 48 min to drive to the park and 39 min to drive home. About how much time did it take Micah's family to drive to and from the park?

_____

5. **Writing in Math** Should you round to the nearest ten or the nearest hundred in order to get the closest estimate? Explain.

_____

_____

PROBLEM-SOLVING SKILL

Writing to Explain

Shells Ned and Mya collected shells on the beach. Ned found 82 shells and Mya found 56 shells. How many more shells did Ned find than Mya?

Read and Understand

1. What are you trying to find?

_____

Plan and Solve

2. Is an exact answer or an estimate needed?

_____

3. What operation should you use? _____

4. Write the answer in a complete sentence.

_____

5. Explain how you found your answer.

_____

Look Back and Check

6. Explain how you can check your answer.

_____

_____

Solve Another Problem

7. Kyle read that there are 170 species of animals at the Little Rock Zoo in Arkansas. Catherine read that there are 229 species of animals at the Miami Metrozoo. About how many fewer species of animals live at the Little Rock Zoo?

PROBLEM-SOLVING APPLICATIONS

How Many Bones?

Bones Babies have 300 bones in their bodies at birth. As people grow, some of the bones fuse together. An adult's body has 206 bones. How many more bones does a baby's body have than an adult's body?

Read and Understand

1. What are you trying to find?

_____

_____

Plan and Solve

2. Which operation will you use? _____

3. Write and solve a number sentence. _____

4. Write the answer in a complete sentence.

_____

Look Back and Check

5. Explain how you can check your answer.

_____

_____

Solve Another Problem

6. Dawson has 372 postcards in his collection. His Aunt Sally sent him 432 postcards that she had collected during her travels. Does he have at least 800 postcards altogether?

_____

Adding Two-Digit Numbers

1. Harley's mother bought a dozen whole-wheat muffins at the market. Then she stopped at the neighborhood bakery to purchase blueberry muffins. She bought a baker's dozen. How many muffins did she purchase in all?

Measurement Chart

dozen	=	12
baker's dozen	=	13
foot	=	12 in.
yard	=	36 in.

_____

2. Sara planted cucumbers in her garden. She planted each cucumber plant 2 ft apart. How many inches apart were Sara's cucumbers? _____

3. At a track-and-field day, Joshua jumped 2 yd and 1 ft in the long jump. How many inches did Joshua jump? _____

4. Austin says 3 ft is the same as 1 yd. Do you agree? Explain.

_____

5. Choose two of the numbers from the list that will have the highest sum, then add.

   49, 27, 34 _____

6. **Writing in Math** Madison counted 43 chickens at her uncle's farm. She also counted 24 turkeys. How many chickens and turkeys did Madison count? Explain how Madison might have estimated the total.

_____

_____

_____

_____

Name_____

Models for Adding Three-Digit Numbers

PS 3-2

1. What problem is shown by these place-value blocks? Write and solve the problem. _____

2. Draw place-value blocks to show 173 + 216. Solve the problem.

3. Cassidy saw 337 fireflies on Monday evening and 248 fireflies on Tuesday evening. How many fireflies did Cassidy see in all? _____

4. To find 635 + 212, George began by combining 3 ones and 2 ones. What did he do wrong?

_____

_____

5. **Writing in Math** Allen wants to show 216 + 358. He has 12 ones blocks. Does he have enough? Explain.

_____

_____

30 Use with Lesson 3-2.

© Pearson Education, Inc. 3

Adding Three-Digit Numbers

1. The Boeing 747 jumbo jet weighs as much as
386 tons at takeoff. It can carry 674 people.
How many people could two of these jets carry? _____

2. How many first- and second-grade
students attend Jackson Elementary?
Find the sum.

_____

Jackson Elementary School	
Grade	Number of Students
1	312
2	279
3	370
4	327
5	296

3. Which two grades have the least
number of students? How many
students do they have combined?

_____

_____

4. Which two grades combined have 682 students?

_____

5. Choose two grade levels and write an addition sentence
that shows regrouping of ones.

_____

6. **Writing in Math** To find the sum of 286 + 134, would you
regroup once or twice? Explain.

_____

_____

_____

Name_____

Adding Three or More Numbers

Nation	Number of Square Miles
Andorra	174
Bahrain	240
Barbados	165
Dominica	290
Grenada	130
Kiribati	280

1. What is the combined square mileage of Andorra, Bahrain, and Barbados? _____

2. What is the combined square mileage of Dominica, Grenada, and Kiribati? _____

3. What is the combined square mileage of the three smallest countries on the chart? _____

4. What is the combined square mileage of the three largest countries on the chart? _____

5. Estimate the combined square mileage of all six countries to the nearest hundred. _____

6. Write an addition problem with three addends. Make the problem so the sum is greater than 400 but less than 600.

_____

7. **Writing in Math** How can you use mental math to find 353 + 50 + 27? Explain.

_____

_____

_____

PROBLEM-SOLVING STRATEGY

Draw a Picture

Ashley and Kirsten washed all 40 tables in the lunchroom. Ashley can wash 3 tables in the same time it takes Kirsten to wash 2 tables. If they washed tables for the same amount of time, how many tables did each girl wash?

Read and Understand

1. How many tables are in the lunchroom? _____

2. How many tables can each girl wash in the same amount of time? _____

_____

3. What are you trying to find?

_____

Plan and Solve

4. Draw a picture to solve the problem. Write your answer in a complete sentence.

_____

_____

Look Back and Check

5. Is your answer reasonable? Explain.

_____

_____

Name_____

Regrouping

1. Give two ways to show $0.63 using nickels and pennies.

_____

_____

2. Give two ways to show $1.00 using quarters and nickels.

_____

_____

3. Draw two ways to show 76 using place-value blocks.

4. Draw two ways to show 238 using place-value blocks.

5. The largest icebergs are found in the Antarctic Ocean, near the South Pole. They can be more than 186 mi long. You can show 186 as 1 hundred, 6 tens, and _____ ones.

6. **Writing in Math** Matthew says 236 = 2 hundreds, 2 tens, 16 ones. Is he correct? Explain.

_____

_____

_____

© Pearson Education, Inc. 3

34 Use with Lesson 3-6.

Name_____

Subtracting Two-Digit Numbers

1. The Cyrillic alphabet, invented in 860, has 32 letters. It is used to write Russian and Bulgarian. How many more letters does the Cyrillic alphabet have than the English alphabet?

_____

2. A full-grown adult has 32 permanent teeth. These permanent teeth are replacements for the 20 teeth children have. How many more teeth does an adult have than a child?

_____

Life Spans The average life spans of some animals are shown on the chart.

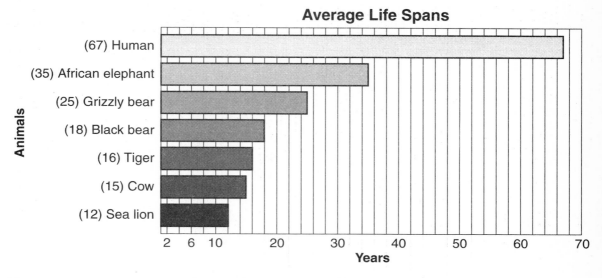

Average Life Spans

Animals: (67) Human, (35) African elephant, (25) Grizzly bear, (18) Black bear, (16) Tiger, (15) Cow, (12) Sea lion

Years: 2 6 10 20 30 40 50 60 70

3. How many more years does a human usually live than a black bear?

_____

4. What is the difference between the life spans of a grizzly bear and a tiger?

_____

5. Two animals have life spans with a difference of 20 years. Which two animals are they?

_____

6. **Writing in Math** Use the chart to write a subtraction problem where you must regroup to solve. Explain your solution.

_____

Models for Subtracting
Three-Digit Numbers

1. Can you subtract 142 from these place-value blocks
   without regrouping? Explain.

   _____

   _____

2. Write and solve a number sentence for Exercise 1.

   _____

3. Draw place-value blocks to show how you would solve 231 − 113.

4. Andy says that to find the difference of 736 − 519 you have
   to regroup twice. Do you agree? Explain.

   _____

   _____

5. **Writing in Math** Write a subtraction problem where you
   need to regroup twice. Explain how you regrouped and
   solved the problem.

   _____

Subtracting Three-Digit Numbers

1. Jennifer's book has 396 pages. She has already
   read 139 pages. How many pages does Jennifer
   have left to read?   _____

2. Alex wants to do 125 sit-ups without stopping.
   Today he did 107 sit-ups. How many more sit-ups
   does Alex have to do to reach his goal?   _____

3. An elephant eats 250 lb of plants a day. If an elephant
   eats 160 lb of plants in the morning, how many more
   pounds of plants will he eat that day?   _____

4. There are 365 days in one year. If 197 days have
   passed since the beginning of the year, how many
   days are left in the year?   _____

5. The fastest train traveled at 252 mi per hour.
   The fastest automobile traveled at 205 mi
   per hour. What is the difference between
   the speeds of the fastest train and the
   fastest automobile?   _____

6. There are 206 bones in the human body. The
   backbone is made up of 33 bones called the
   vertebrae. How many of the body's bones are
   not vertebrae?   _____

7. **Writing in Math** Write a three-digit subtraction problem
   with a difference of 308. Explain how you figured out the
   numbers in the problem.

   _____

   _____

   _____

   _____

Name_____

Subtracting Across Zero

1. Heather's book has 100 pages. She has 37 pages left to read. How many pages has Heather already read?

_____

2. Mrs. Healy's class needs 250 points to earn their next field trip. They have already earned 107 points. How many points do they still need to earn?

_____

3. A box of paper has 500 sheets. Mr. Paton's class used 426 sheets of paper during the last six months. How many sheets are left in the box? _____

4. The Sears Tower in Chicago, Illinois, has 110 stories. The Jin Mao Building in Shanghai, China, has 88 stories. How many stories taller is the Sears Tower? _____

Everglades Everglades National Park is home to 300 species of birds, 120 kinds of trees, and 25 types of orchids.

5. Mikayla was able to find 87 different trees during a two-day hike with her family. How many more trees can she find?

_____

6. How many more types of trees are there than types of orchids?

_____

7. Badlands National Park has 56 species of grass. Is this more or less than the kinds of trees found in Everglades National Park? Write a number sentence to show your answer.

_____

8. **Writing in Math** Write your own word problem about the birds that live in the Everglades. Then solve the problem.

_____

_____

_____

PROBLEM-SOLVING SKILL
Exact Answer or Estimate?

Coat Drive The third-grade classes collected used coats and jackets to give to a clothing drive. Their goal was to collect at least 55 coats. Did they meet their goal?

Coat Drive	
Class	**Number of Coats**
3 A	OOOOOOOOOOOO
3 B	OOOOOOOOO▢
3 C	OOOOOOOOOO▢

Each O = 2 coats.
Each ▢ = 1 coat.

Read and Understand

1. How many coats were collected by each class?

_____

2. What are you trying to find?

_____

Plan and Solve

3. Is an estimate enough? Explain.

_____

4. Solve the problem. Write your answer in a complete sentence.

_____

Look Back and Check

5. How do you know your estimate is reasonable?

_____

_____

Name_____

Adding and Subtracting Money

1. Hillary paid a $3.75 admission fee to tour the zoo. She paid with a $5.00 bill. How much change did she get?

   _____

2. Hillary ate lunch at the zoo's snack shop. She paid $1.98 for a ham sandwich and $1.03 for a large fruit juice. How much money did she spend for lunch?

   _____

3. Hillary would like to treat her younger brother and sister to a day at the zoo. How much will she have to save to pay for all three admissions?

   _____

Gift Shop Hillary stopped at the zoo's gift shop before returning home. The chart shows a price list of items for sale.

Elephant puzzle	$3.95
Postcard pack	$1.87
Lion mug	$2.89
Zoo blocks	$4.80
Monkey puppet	$3.75

4. Hillary paid for the postcard pack with two $1.00 bills. How much change did she get?

   _____

5. How much would a monkey puppet and zoo blocks cost?

   _____

6. If a customer paid for 2 items with a $10.00 bill and had $2.31 left over, what 2 items did he buy?

   _____

7. **Writing in Math** Joe estimates that since he has only $5.00, he can't buy 2 different items as gifts for his parents. Do you agree with his estimate? Explain.

   _____

   _____

   _____

Choose a Computation Method

1. Tell how you could use mental math to solve 368 − 199.

_____

_____

_____

Languages Many different languages are spoken all over the world. The most widely spoken languages are shown on the table.

2. How many people speak English and Spanish? What computation method did you use?

_____

_____

World Languages

Language	Number of People (in millions)
Mandarin Chinese	885
Hindustani	461
English	450
Spanish	352

3. How many more people speak Hindustani than Spanish? What computation method did you use?

_____

4. **Writing in Math** Explain when you would choose to use a calculator to solve a math problem.

_____

_____

_____

Name_____

Equality and Inequality

1. Krista, Carol, and Ben all solved the problem $1 + 7 < 10 -$ _____.
   Krista says the answer is 1. Carol says the answer is 2. Ben
   says the answer is 0. Are their answers correct? Explain.

   _____

   _____

   _____

   _____

2. Find three whole numbers that make $106 + x > 212$ true.

   _____

   _____

3. Harper thinks there is more than one whole number that
   will make $16 - x = 9$ true. Do you agree? Explain.

   _____

   _____

4. The number sentence $17 + 2 = 15$ is false. Find two ways
   you could change it to make it true.

   _____

5. **Writing in Math** Write a number sentence that makes the
   expressions $11 + x$ and $16 - 3$ equal. Explain how you
   would find what numbers and symbols would make it true.

   _____

   _____

   _____

Name_____

Leaf Collection

Mikel spent $13.19 on supplies to display his leaf collection. He paid for the supplies with a $10.00 bill, a $5.00 bill, and a quarter. How much money did he have left?

Read and Understand

1. How much did Mikel spend?   _____

2. How much did Mikel use to pay for the supplies?   _____

3. What are you trying to find?

   _____

Plan and Solve

4. Write a number sentence and solve the problem.

   _____

5. Write the answer in a complete sentence.

   _____

Look Back and Check

6. Explain how you can check your answer.

   _____

   _____

Solve Another Problem

7. Alaskan fur seals travel as far as 3,200 km south each autumn. Monarch butterflies travel to southern parts of North America, often traveling 1,600 km. How many more kilometers do fur seals travel than monarch butterflies?

   _____

Time to the Half Hour and Quarter Hour

A Great Book Timothy was reading a book about dinosaurs. It was 6:30 P.M. when he started reading. His bedtime was at 8:00 P.M.

1. Draw a clock face with the hands showing the time Timothy started reading.

2. Draw a clock face with the hands showing Timothy's bedtime.

3. Timothy finished reading chapter 9 at the time shown. Write the time in two ways.

_____

4. Writing in Math Timothy wakes up for school at the time shown. Write the time Timothy wakes up in two different ways using words.

_____

_____

Time to the Minute

One Saturday Mr. and Mrs. Adams went out for dinner and a movie at twenty-five after six. They arrived home at ten thirty-three.

1. Write the time Mr. and Mrs. Adams left for the evening in number form.

   _____

2. Write the time they came home in two different ways.

   _____

3. Draw two clock faces with the hands showing the times Mr. and Mrs. Adams left and came home.

4. **Writing in Math** The clock shows the time Bart gets home from school. Write the time in three different ways.

   _____

   _____

Elapsed Time

First Plane Trip Bob recently took his first airplane ride. He departed from New York City at 8:00 A.M. and arrived in Detroit, Michigan, at 9:50 A.M.

1. How long was the airplane ride?

   _____

2. On the return flight a week later, Bob departed from Detroit at 7:10 A.M. and arrived in New York City 1 hr and 40 min later. What time did he arrive?

   _____

3. How much shorter was Bob's return trip?

   _____

4. Susan flew from New York City all the way to Miami, Florida. The actual flying time was 3 hr and 15 min. If she left New York City on the 11:00 A.M. flight, what was her expected arrival time?

   _____

5. **Writing in Math** Juanita and Elizabeth have a softball game at 10:00 A.M. If it takes them 15 min to get home and the game lasts 1 hr 40 min, at what time will they get home? Explain.

   _____

   _____

   _____

   _____

Name_____

Using a Calendar

A full Moon occurs once each month. In August the full Moon was seen on the 22nd.

August 2002						
S	M	T	W	T	F	S
				1	2	3
4	5	6	7	8	9	10
11	12	13	14	15	16	17
18	19	20	21	22	23	24
25	26	27	28	29	30	31

September 2002						
S	M	T	W	T	F	S
1	2	3	4	5	6	7
8	9	10	11	12	13	14
15	16	17	18	19	20	21
22	23	24	25	26	27	28
29	30					

1. What day of the week was the 22nd of August in the year 2002?

   _____

2. If the Moon was a crescent shape 1 week after the full Moon, on what day and date would that be?

   _____

3. Jamille started working on a school project on August 20, 2002. He finished 3 weeks and 5 days later. What day of the week and date did Jamille finish?

   _____

The Tosilito family went on vacation to San Francisco, California, on September 25, 2002. The family returned from vacation 6 days later.

4. **Writing in Math** Use the calendar to figure out the day and the date of the Tosilito family's return. Explain your answer.

   _____

   _____

   _____

   _____

   _____

Using Tally Charts to Organize Data PS 4-5

Favorite Subject Cheryl took a survey of third graders that asked, "What is your favorite subject in school?" She recorded the data using a tally chart.

Favorite Subject		
Subject	**Tally Marks**	**Number**
Math	⊬⊬	5
Science	⊬⊬ |||	8
Art	⊬⊬		6
Gym	||||	4
Music	||	2
Spelling	|||	3

1. How many third graders were surveyed?

_____

2. How many more third graders voted for science than spelling?

_____

3. What number is shown by ⊬⊬ ⊬⊬ ⊬⊬? _____

Salvatore kept track of how many times people said "please," "thank you," or "you're welcome" during lunch at the cafeteria counter.

> you're welcome, thank you, please, thank you, thank you, please, please, please, thank you, you're welcome, thank you, thank you, thank you, please, please, you're welcome, thank you, thank you, please

4. **Writing in Math** Use the data to complete the tally chart. Then tell which phrase was used most often. What was the total number of times it was used?

Salvatore's Survey

Polite Phrase	Tally	Number
Please		
Thank you		
You're welcome		

Using Line Plots to Organize Data

Test Scores A third-grade class took a math test on addition and subtraction facts. The teacher, Ms. Bartlett, made a line plot to help her compare the scores of her students.

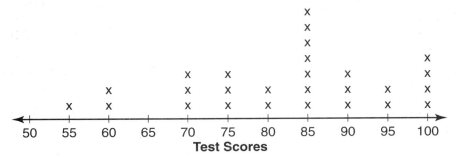

1. How many students scored 85 or better? _____

2. How many students scored below 85? _____

3. What is the range and mode of the data?

_____

Family Sizes Each student in a third-grade class painted their family portrait for an art assignment. They made a line plot to show how many people were in each family.

Number of Family Members

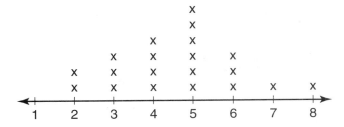

4. How many families had 5 people or more? _____

5. **Writing in Math** What is the mean for the family sizes of 12, 8, 6, 5, and 4 people? Explain your answer.

_____

_____

Reading Pictographs and Bar Graphs PS 4-7

Today, there are many different types of phones for sale. The bar graph shows the number of different types of phones sold in one month at Abe's Communication Store.

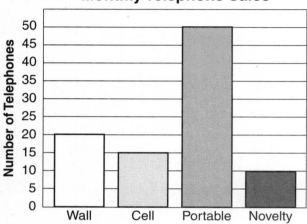

Monthly Telephone Sales

1. How many phones were sold for the month? _____

2. How many more portable phones were sold than wall phones? _____

3. Of the novelty phones, 2 were shaped like cars and 6 were shaped like basketballs. The rest were shaped like an animal. How many phones were shaped like an animal?

_____

4. **Writing in Math** Write a comparison problem that can be solved by using the graph and answer it.

_____

_____

_____

_____

Name_____

Writing to Compare

Which city had a greater number of days of snow or rainfall throughout the months?

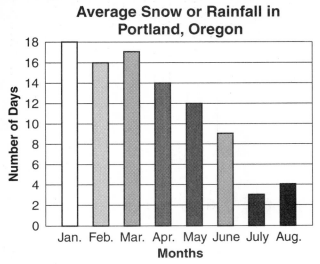

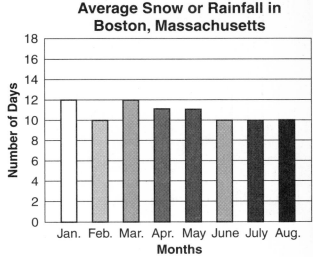

Read and Understand

1. What are you trying to find?

_____

_____

Plan and Solve

2. Answer the question and explain.

_____

_____

_____

Look Back and Check

3. Is your answer reasonable based on the graphs?

_____

_____

Graphing Ordered Pairs

Partners The students in a third-grade class made a coordinate grid for the location of some of their houses near the school.

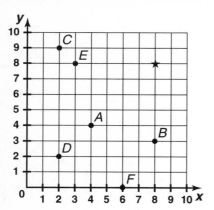

1. Give the ordered pair for the houses at point *C* and point *F.*

   _____

2. Is the ordered pair (3, 8) correct for the house located at point *B?* Explain your answer.

   _____

   _____

   _____

3. The star represents the location of the school. What is its ordered pair?

   _____

4. **Writing in Math** Sue says the points (1, 3), (1, 5), (3, 5), and (3, 3) can be connected to make a square. Is she correct? Explain.

   _____

   _____

   _____

Reading Line Graphs

The line graph shows the average days of rain or snow for New York City.

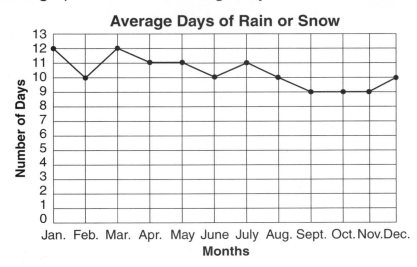

Average Days of Rain or Snow

1. On average, how many more days of rain or snow are there in January than in December?

_____

2. Which 3 months have 11 days of rain or snow?

_____

The line graph shows the number of videos Thad's video store rented each day during one week.

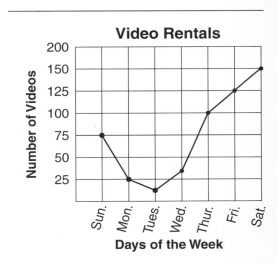

Video Rentals

3. List the days in order from the greatest number of video rentals to the least number of video rentals.

_____

_____

_____

4. **Writing in Math** Thad wants to close the store one day per week. Based on the information in the graph, which day would you recommend? Explain your reasoning.

_____

Making Pictographs

Favorite Music A fifth-grade class was discussing what type of music was most popular. They could not agree, so they decided to take a survey.

1. Complete the tally chart.

Type of Music	Tally	Number
Rap	卌 I	
Country	卌 卌	
Pop	卌 卌 II	
Rock	卌 II	
R & B	卌 I	

2. Use the data from the tally chart to complete the pictograph.

Favorite Music	
Rap	
Country	
Pop	
Rock	
R&B	

Each ♪ = 2 people.

3. How many students were surveyed in all?

_____

4. **Writing in Math** Explain how you know which type of music is the most popular.

_____

_____

Making Bar Graphs

Family Vacation The Cortez family took a vacation by car.
They drove through 4 different states. The drive through
Michigan totaled 375 mi. They traveled 200 mi through Ohio
and 400 mi across Pennsylvania. They drove 180 mi through
New York.

1. Complete the bar graph using the data given above.

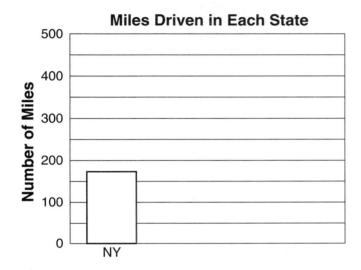

2. Which state does the shortest bar represent?

_____

3. How many miles did the Cortez family cover altogether?

_____

4. **Writing in Math** Explain how you can best use a bar graph.

_____

_____

_____

Name_____

Making Line Graphs

The third-grade teacher, Ms. Stigler, gave each student a "multiplication mad minute" at the beginning of each math class on Monday to test the student's mastery of multiplication tables. Each student had 1 min to solve 50 problems. Ms. Stigler kept the data in a notebook. To the right is the data for the first 8 weeks of the semester.

Average Test Scores	
Week 1—70%	Week 5—78%
Week 2—74%	Week 6—80%
Week 3—72%	Week 7—82%
Week 4—80%	Week 8—90%

1. Make a line graph using grid paper.

2. Which week had the lowest average score? Which week had the highest average score?

_____

3. **Writing in Math** What changes occurred between Week 1 and Week 8? Why do you think those changes occurred?

_____

_____

_____

_____

PROBLEM-SOLVING STRATEGY
Make a Graph

Mr. Johnston made a table for one week to show the principal the number of students that attended the homework-help room.

How did the number of students change over the week?

Monday	5
Tuesday	4
Wednesday	4
Thursday	10
Friday	2

Read and Understand

1. How many students attended the homework-help room each day?

   _____

2. What are you trying to find?

   _____

Plan and Solve

3. Would you use a bar graph, a pictograph, or a line graph to help find your answer? _____

4. Make the graph.

Look Back and Check

5. Does your graph give you the information you need to answer the question? _____

PROBLEM-SOLVING APPLICATIONS   **PS 4-15**
Lemonade Stand

Four children had lemonade stands. The lemonade at each stand
cost $0.25 for each glass. The chart shows their sales for one week.

	Monday	Tuesday	Wednesday	Thursday	Friday
Kelly	$5	$4	$6	$7	$5
Antonio	$2	$3	$1	$1	$3
Bill	$6	$4	$6	$4	$10
Sue	$4	$1	$3	$2	$3

Use a graph to show who had the best total sales for the week.

Read and Understand

1. What are you trying to show?

_____

Plan and Solve

2. First, find the total sales for each child.

_____

3. Complete
   the graph.

4. Who had
   the best
   total sales?

   _____

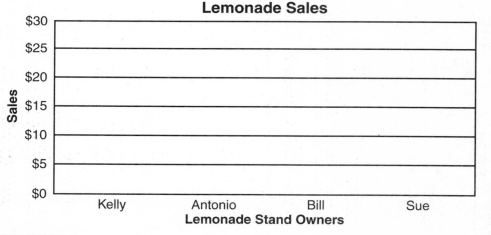

Look Back and Check

5. Did you make the best graph choice? How do you know?

_____

Multiplication as Repeated Addition   PS 5-1

Insects are an important and useful part of our everyday life. They provide food for other animals and pollinate flowers and forests. Insects come in many different shapes and colors, but all insects have 6 legs. Each insect also has 2 antennae, or feelers. Ants and dragonflies are two examples of insects.

1. What is the total number of legs on 2 dragonflies and 2 ants?

_____

2. How many antennae would there be in a group of 10 ants?

_____

3. Write an addition sentence and a multiplication sentence for the number of legs on a group of 4 ants.

_____

Firefly is another name for lightning bug. It is a member of the beetle family. The firefly has 2 pairs of wings. The first pair of wings is used to cover the second pair of wings. The second pair of wings is used for flying.

4. Write a multiplication sentence for the number of wings on 3 fireflies.

_____

5. **Writing in Math** Is the following statement true or false? Explain your answer. Use both an addition and a multiplication sentence for your answer.

   2 groups of 3 fireflies have a total of 24 wings.

_____

_____

_____

_____

_____

Arrays and Multiplication

Model T The Model T was the first car made by Henry Ford's motor company in 1908. The car cost $825.00 and, at the time, this was more than most people could afford. To help lower the cost of the car, Ford developed an assembly-line system. By 1924 the Ford Model T cost only $290.00. Most families could then afford to own their first car.

1. If there were 5 houses on each block in the early 1900s and all of the homes had Model T cars, how many cars would there be on 2 blocks?

_____

2. Use the Commutative Property of Multiplication to write two different multiplication sentences for Exercise 1.

_____

Electric Cars Electric cars are powered by rechargeable batteries instead of gasoline. Therefore, they do not produce air pollution. Why are there only a few electric cars on the road? At this time, the problem is that electric cars can only travel about 100 mi before the battery needs to be recharged.

3. The car dealership could not decide how to display its 6 new electric cars. Draw two different arrays for the cars.

4. Write the multiplication sentences that would match the two different arrays you drew for Exercise 3.

_____

5. **Writing in Math** Write your own problem using cars to show the Commutative Property of Multiplication.

_____

Writing Multiplication Stories

Brenna had a party for 5 friends. Her mom made a party favor bag for each friend. Each bag contained 4 pencils, 2 toys, and 3 stickers.

1. How many pencils did Brenna's mom
   need to buy to fill the 5 party-favor bags? _____

2. How many stickers and toys did Brenna's mom need to
   buy to fill the 5 party-favor bags?

   _____

3. How many party favors did Brenna's mom buy altogether?
   How do you know this is a multiplication story?

   _____

   _____

At Brenna's party, there was also a piñata filled with stamps in the shapes of animals. The animal shapes were a zebra, an elephant, a cow, and a horse.

4. Jillian broke the piñata. She found 3 stamps
   of each kind of animal. How many stamps
   did she find? _____

5. **Writing in Math** Write a multiplication story about Brenna's
   party. Draw a picture for your story. Solve the problem.

   _____

   _____

   _____

Name_____

Make a Table

Kathleen's aunt was having a cookout. Kathleen helped her set up the tables. She put a glass of water next to each plate. There were 6 plates at each table. There were 8 tables in the backyard. How many glasses of water did Kathleen need for the 8 tables?

Read and Understand

1. What are you trying to find?

   _____

   _____

Plan and Solve

2. How many glasses did she place at the
   first table? How many total glasses did
   she place after the second table?   _____

3. Finish the table to help solve the problem.

Number of Tables	1	2	3	4	5	6	7	8
Number of Glasses	6	12						

4. Write your answer in a complete sentence.

   _____

   _____

Look Back and Check

5. Explain how the table helped you solve the problem.

   _____

   _____

2 as a Factor

The Virginia Reel and the Morris Dance are two different types of square dancing.

1. To start the Virginia Reel, partners line up facing each other. Ten students lined up to learn the Virginia Reel. An equal number of students formed a second line, facing them. How many students were in both lines?

_____

2. In the Morris Dance, teams of 6 men are set up in 2 rows of 3. Below is a picture of 4 groups of dancers. Using 2 as a factor for multiplying, write a multiplication sentence that tells how many dancers there are.

Morris Dancers

_____

A gym teacher decided to teach ballroom dancing to the class. The teacher put students into pairs to begin teaching the steps.

3. If there were 8 pairs, how many students participated?

_____

4. The ballroom dance took 3 min to complete. If they did the dance 2 separate times how much time would it take them? _____

5. **Writing in Math** How many students were participating in a dance if there were 16 pairs of dancers? Explain how you found your answer.

_____

_____

5 as a Factor

Homework Kelsey was assigned math homework. He was given 8 word problems to solve. He estimated that it would take him 5 min to solve each problem.

1. How much time would it take Kelsey to complete his math homework?   _____

2. Write a multiplication sentence for Exercise 1. Show skip counting as another way to solve the problem.

_____

3. What two factors would show how it could take Kelsey an hour to complete 12 problems at 5 min per problem?   _____

School Supplies The school store was having a clearance sale on supplies. Marge needed to buy more school supplies for the rest of the school year. She had $5.00 to spend.

Notebooks	$0.40
Pens	$0.30
Erasers	$0.10
Pencils	$0.20

4. How much would it cost Marge to buy 5 pencils and 5 erasers? How much change would she get back from her $5.00 bill?

_____

5. **Writing in Math** Could Marge buy 5 of each item on sale at the store? Explain.

_____

_____

_____

10 as a Factor

Race Seth and Janice ran in a 10-km race. There were 7 other runners at the starting line with Seth and Janice. Seth usually ran a kilometer in 4 min, and Janice usually ran a kilometer in 5 min.

1. How many runners in total were at the starting line? If all of the runners finished the race, how many kilometers combined did they run?

_____

2. If Janice ran in her usual time, how long would it take her to finish the race? _____

3. If both Seth and Janice run their usual times, who would finish the race first? Write two multiplication sentences you can use to answer the question.

_____

Parade Day At the Independence Day Parade, Clarence the Clown had 10 each of 10 different colored buttons that said "smile." On every block that he marched in the parade, he gave out 10 buttons.

4. How many "smile" buttons did Clarence give out after marching 5 blocks in the parade? _____

5. **Writing in Math** Use the picture to write a multiplication story. Write a multiplication sentence and solve the problem.

_____

_____

_____

_____

PROBLEM-SOLVING SKILL

Multiple-Step Problems

Long Distance Philip and his brother José each made a long distance call to a friend who had moved to another state. Philip spoke for 10 min and José spoke for 5 min. Their long distance phone plan charged $0.10 per minute. How much did the boys spend altogether?

Read and Understand

1. How long was each boy on the phone?

   _____

2. What was the cost of their telephone plan?

   _____

3. What are you trying to find out?

   _____

Plan and Solve

4. What is one of the hidden questions?

   _____

5. One way to solve the problem is to add the total minutes of each boy's call, then multiply by $0.10. What is another way to solve the problem?

   _____

   _____

6. What is the total cost of the calls?   _____

Look Back and Check

7. Did you get the same answer for both methods of solving the problem?   _____

Name_____

Multiplying with 0 and 1

The Cronin family would like to go to a circus that was in town, but they need to check out the ticket prices. A ticket for a child is $1.00, and a ticket for an adult is $5.00.

1. How much will it cost for the 4 Cronin children's tickets?

_____

2. A senior citizen's ticket costs the same as a child's ticket. How much will it cost for 7 senior citizens to attend the circus?

_____

3. It costs $1.00 for popcorn at the circus. If the circus sold 857 bags of popcorn, how much money did they make?

_____

Kate loves to garden. This year Kate planted the seeds for 4 tomato plants, 3 cucumber plants, and 2 green pepper plants. There was very little rain this summer. In August Kate found the tomato plant had only green tomatoes, the cucumber plant had flowers but no cucumbers, and there were no green peppers at all.

4. How many red ripe tomatoes was Kate able to harvest? Write a multiplication sentence for this problem.

_____

5. Write a number sentence for the total number of ripe vegetables Kate harvested in August.

_____

6. Writing in Math The product of two numbers is zero. One of the factors is zero. Explain why both 17 and 342 are correct answers for the other factor.

_____

_____

_____

9 as a Factor

The Iditarod race takes place in Alaska. The object of the race is to see which musher and dogs can cover the race in the shortest amount of time. At least 5 dogs must pull the sled to the finish line.

1. If a race had 9 teams with 6 dogs each and 7 teams with 9 dogs each, how many teams participated? _____

2. How many dogs would be in the race? _____

3. Each musher must bring 8 booties for each dog in the race. If the musher has 9 dogs on his team, how many booties should he have altogether? _____

Patty walks 9 groups of dogs each day. There are 4 dogs in each group.

4. How many dogs does Patty walk in all each day? _____

5. **Writing in Math** Explain how the picture of the fingers shows the answer to the problem 9 × 5.

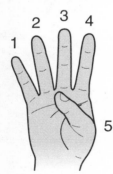 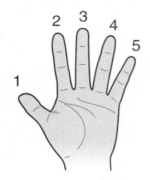

_____

_____

_____

_____

Practicing Multiplication Facts

Library Day Once a week the students at North School visit the library. Each student in kindergarten and first grade checks out 1 book each week. Each student in second grade through fourth grade checks out 2 books each week. The fifth and sixth grade students each check out 3 books a week.

1. If 9 first-grade students, 2 fourth-grade students, and 4 fifth-grade students went to the library, how many books would they check out in all? _____

2. The librarian found that there were many books about caring for pets. There were 9 books each about dogs, cats, birds, fish, and rabbits. How many books were there about caring for pets altogether? _____

Zoo A class of third graders took a field trip to the zoo. On the bus, the students sat in groups of 4 with 1 adult chaperone. There were 6 groups in all.

3. How many students went to the zoo? _____

4. How many students and chaperones went to the zoo altogether?

   _____

5. **Writing in Math** Explain how knowing that $12 \times 10 = 120$ could help you find the product of 12×5.

   _____

   _____

   _____

   _____

   _____

Name_____

Sidewalk Sale

A music store is having a sidewalk sale. All CDs are on sale at low prices for one day only. Any CDs that have a damaged case are on sale for $5. Any used CDs are on sale for $10. Lastly, all new CDs are on sale for $15. Calista has picked out 5 CDs with damaged cases, 1 new CD, and 1 used CD. How much will she pay altogether?

Read and Understand

1. How much does each type of CD cost?

   _____

2. How many of each type of CD did Calista pick out?

   _____

3. What are you trying to find?

   _____

Plan and Solve

4. What operations will you use to solve the problem?

   _____

5. Solve the problem and write the answer in a complete sentence.

   _____

Look Back and Check

6. Explain why you can use counting by 5s and 10s to check your answer.

   _____

   _____

3 as a Factor

Admission Jeni's family is going to the State Fair. Jeni and her 2 sisters will pay the child's price for admission, but her mom, dad, and 14-year-old brother will have to pay the adult's price.

Welcome to the STATE FAIR	
Admissions	**Price**
Adult	$8.00
Child (Ages 4–12)	$5.00
Under Age 4	FREE!
"Ride-All-Day" .... wristbands	$12.00

1. How much will the family pay for Jeni and her 2 sisters?

   _____

2. How much will the family pay for the 3 adult admissions?

   _____

3. What will the family's total cost be for admission to the fair?

   _____

4. No matter what a person's age, the price of a "Ride-All-Day" wristband is always the same. What is the cost of 3 wristbands?

   _____

5. In 1998, 3 sets of triplets were born within 4 days at University Hospital in Cincinnati. How many babies were born?

   _____

6. There are 3 ft in a yard. How many feet are there in 11 yd?

   _____

7. **Writing in Math** Explain how you can solve Exercise 6 using two different arrays.

   _____

   _____

   _____

   _____

Name_____

4 as a Factor

Car Repairs A corner car repair shop uses 4 lug nuts per tire to fasten each tire rim to a hub.

1. Simon replaced all 4 tires on a car. How many lug nuts did he use?

   _____

2. Jolie had 4 cars to repair but each car had only 2 tires to replace. How many lug nuts did she use?

   _____

3. The festival downtown ended with a competition of quartets. Each quartet was made up of 4 singers. There were 9 groups competing. How many singers competed?

   _____

4. Each side of a square has a measurement of 8 in. What is the measurement of all 4 sides?

   _____

5. The Anderson Speedway in Indiana is an oval track for racing cars. Each completed trip around the track is called a lap. To complete a mile, a racer must go around the track 4 times. How many laps will the racer complete in a 3-mi race?

   _____

6. Sandy just bought a new table and 6 chairs. Each chair has 4 legs, and the table has 4 legs. She wants to put felt pads on each leg to keep them from scratching the floor. How many felt pads does Sandy need?

   _____

7. **Writing in Math** Juanita says that to find 4×6, she can double the product of 2×3. Is she correct? Explain.

   _____

   _____

6 and 7 as Factors

1. Rachel is making uniform shirts for her son's baseball team. Each shirt has 6 buttons. There are 12 players on the team. How many buttons does Rachel need? _____

2. A school grading period is 10 weeks. How many days are in the grading period, including the weekends? _____

3. On a pair of athletic shoes, there are 6 eyelets on one side of one shoe. How many total eyelets are there on 3 pairs of shoes? Use 5s facts and 1s facts to show your answer.

_____

_____

Camera Rodger gets $7 a week in allowance. He is saving all his money to buy a new digital camera. The camera costs $160.

4. At the end of 4 weeks, how much will Rodger have saved? _____

5. If Rodger saves all his allowance for 7 weeks, how much money will he have saved? Use breaking apart into 5s facts and 2s facts to show your answer.

_____

6. Rodger has saved his allowance for 10 weeks now, but each week he has spent $1 of his allowance. How much money does Rodger still need to save to buy the camera? _____

7. **Writing in Math** Explain two ways you could find the product of 6×7.

_____

_____

_____

8 as a Factor

1. Carey collects action figures. He needs
   3 more figures to complete a set. Each
   figure costs $8. How much does Carey
   need to spend in order to complete the set?   _____

2. A computer printer can print 8 pages of
   color printing in 1 min. How many pages
   can the same printer print in 9 min?   _____

3. Pine boards come in 8-ft long sections.
   If you are putting up a fence that needs
   7 boards, how long would the fence be?   _____

Book Club Teresa is cooking breakfast for her book club.
There are 8 members.

4. If Teresa is cooking 2 eggs for each club
   member, how many eggs would she need?   _____

5. Teresa plans to get 6 oz of juice for each
   member. How much juice does she need?   _____

6. **Writing in Math** A garden is made up of 8 rose plants
   arranged in 8 rows. Draw the rose garden as an array of 4
   $\times$ 8 doubled. How many rose plants are there in the
   garden? How is this a square number?

_____

_____

Name_____

Practicing Multiplication Facts

Food Pyramid The United States Department of Agriculture (USDA) has created a food pyramid to help people know the types and amounts of foods they should eat.

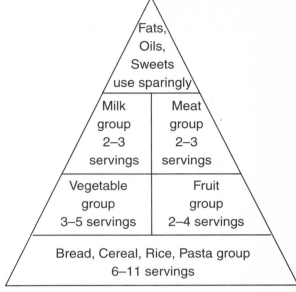

1. A typical serving from the vegetable group is 1 c of a green leafy vegetable. How many cups of any vegetable are necessary to fill the minimum daily requirements?

   _____

2. You can substitute 2 oz of processed cheese for a 1 c serving of milk. How many ounces of processed cheese do you need to eat to provide the minimum number of servings?

   _____

3. The USDA also suggests that an average person should drink 8 glasses of water each day. If each glass is 8 oz, how many ounces of water should an average person drink each day?

   _____

4. **Writing in Math** A serving from the meat group is 2 oz. If you ate 3 servings a day, how many ounces would you eat in a week? Explain how you found your answer using 3 methods: Commutative Property, 5s facts, and doubling.

   _____

   _____

   _____

   _____

   _____

Name_____

Look for a Pattern

New Sidewalk Every day, Tara has been watching the workers build a new sidewalk on her street. Each day she has counted the number of new sections added to the sidewalk. She has found a pattern. If the pattern continues, how many sections will the workers have built by the end of the 6th day?

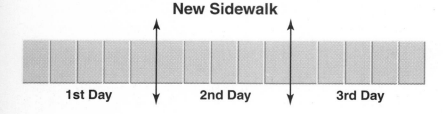

New Sidewalk

1st Day   2nd Day   3rd Day

Read and Understand

1. How many sidewalk sections are built each day? _____

2. What are you trying to find?

   _____

   _____

Plan and Solve

3. Find the pattern.

   _____

   _____

4. Extend the pattern for 6 days. Solve the problem.

   _____

Look Back and Check

5. Check your answer using another method.

   _____

Using Multiplication to Compare

Buying in Bulk Jordan's mother likes to buy certain items in bulk. When she compares the number of items in a bulk package to those in a regular package, she always finds that she can save money by buying in bulk.

1. A regular-sized package of paper towels has 2 rolls of paper towels. The bulk package contains 6 times that many. How many rolls of paper towels are in the bulk package? _____

2. Health food bars are normally sold in a package of 4 bars. The bulk package has 8 times that amount. How many health food bars are in the bulk pack? _____

3. A regular-sized package of boxes of facial tissue contains 3 boxes. The bulk size has 2 times as many. How many tissue boxes are in the bulk package? _____

Crayons Ben needs to buy crayons for the new school year. He can buy an 8-color package for $1.00, or a package with 3 times as many crayons for $1.99.

4. How many crayons are in the larger package? _____

5. How much would it cost to buy 3 of the crayon packages that contain 8 colors? _____

6. **Writing in Math** Margaret has 8 red beads. Draw a picture to show she has 3 times as many white beads as red beads. Explain how the picture helps you use multiplication to compare.

_____

_____

Patterns on a Table

Vet Day Barb works for a veterinarian. Her job is to keep track of how many animals are brought into the office and what their treatment is. She is also in charge of keeping track of how much money is owed to the doctor.

1. If 9 cats received distemper shots, and each treatment is made up of 2 shots, how many shots were given? _____

2. An office visit for an illness costs $8. How much money did it cost for the week if 3 ill birds were brought in on Monday, 2 on Tuesday, and 1 each on Wednesday, Thursday, and Friday? _____

3. For each of the 4 dogs that were immunized on Wednesday, Barb had to fill out 5 forms. For each of the 5 injured snakes that were also brought in on Wednesday, she had to fill out 4 forms. How many forms did Barb fill out altogether? _____

Hatchery Amber ordered eggs for her incubator. She ordered 8 each of 3 different kinds of chicken eggs, 6 each of 2 types of duck eggs, and 40 pheasant eggs.

4. How many chicken eggs did Amber order? _____

5. How many eggs did Amber order altogether? _____

6. **Writing in Math** Amber decided to order several different types of pheasant eggs. Give 4 different combinations that could equal the 40 eggs she ordered.

_____

_____

_____

_____

Multiplying with Three Factors

1. If a bookseller in Chicago wraps every 2 books together in bubble wrap, then packages them into small boxes that contain 2 bubble-wrap packs each, and then into cartons that will hold 6 small boxes, how many books will the bookseller send out in each carton?

   _____

2. A parking lot is arranged in rows with 2 cars back to back and 5 cars across. If there are 4 rows, how many cars can park in the lot?

   _____

3. There are 2 c in a pint, 2 pt in a quart, and 4 qt in a gallon. How many cups are there in a gallon?

   _____

4. Kathy multiplied $3 \times 4 \times 5$ this way.

   Using the Associative Property of Multiplication, show another way Kathy could have multiplied $3 \times 4 \times 5$.

   Kathy's Solution

$3 \times 4 \times 5 =$
$12 \times 5 =$
60

5. **Writing in Math** An orange grower packages his premium oranges in crates of 3 layers. Each layer is 3 oranges wide and 2 oranges long. How many oranges are sent out in a crate? Draw a picture that represents a crate and write a multiplication sentence that answers the question.

   _____

   _____

Find a Rule

Speed Different types of helicopters fly at different speeds. A traffic helicopter might stay in one place for long periods of time, while a transport helicopter will move quickly. The average speed of a helicopter is shown in the table.

Minutes	1	2	3	4	5
Distance in Miles	2	4	6		

1. How many miles will a helicopter travel in 1 min? In 2 min?   _____

2. Write a multiplication rule that will work for the helicopter-speed table.   _____

3. How many miles will the helicopter travel in 5 min?   _____

4. How many miles will it travel in 9 min?   _____

5. Every week Dion spends $3 on dog treats for his collie, Mambo. By the 4th week he has spent $12 on Mambo's treats. In what week will he have spent $21 total?   _____

6. **Writing in Math** Explain a different pattern for Mambo's treats where Dion spends $21.

_____

_____

_____

_____

_____

_____

PROBLEM-SOLVING SKILL   **PS 6-11**

Choose an Operation

House Lights Alex turned off 7 lights around his house, but 3 were still on. How many lights were on before Alex turned them off?

Read and Understand

1. How many lights did Alex turn off?   _____

2. How many lights were still on?   _____

Plan and Solve

3. Draw a picture to show the main idea.

4. What operation should you use?   _____

5. Write the answer in a complete sentence.

_____

_____

Look Back and Check

6. Explain how you can check your answer.

_____

_____

_____

_____

Name_____

PROBLEM-SOLVING APPLICATIONS

Paper Weights

PS 6-12

Tomas purchases computer paper in boxes that contain 2,500 sheets of paper. Each box weighs 20 lb. The cart Tomas uses says, "Do not load this cart with more than 100 lb." How many boxes of paper can Tomas put on his cart?

Read and Understand

1. What extra information is given?

_____

2. How much does each box of paper weigh? _____

3. What are you trying to find?

_____

_____

Plan and Solve

4. Complete the table.

Number of Boxes	1	2	3	4	5
Weight in Pounds	20	40			

5. Write the answer in a complete sentence.

_____

_____

Look Back and Check

6. Explain how you can check your answer.

_____

_____

_____

82 Use with Lesson 6-12.

© Pearson Education, Inc. 3

Division as Sharing

1. Suppose a female cat had a litter of 6 kittens. The owners wanted 2 of their friends to share the kittens equally. How many kittens did each friend receive?

   _____

2. The Johnson's family cat had a litter of 8 kittens. They kept 2 kittens and gave the others equally to 3 different people. How many kittens did each of the 3 people receive?

   _____

3. Susan raises 3 different types of cats: tabbies, angoras, and calicos. Currently she has 9 cats. There are equal numbers of each type. How many of each type does she have? Draw a picture that shows how you solved the problem.

   _____

4. Dr. Raymond treats cats in her 3 veterinary clinics. She has 24 cats in the clinics. If there are an equal number of cats in each clinic, how many cats are in each one?

   _____

5. **Writing in Math** If Dr. Raymond opens a 4th clinic and brings an equal number of cats to each one, how many cats will there be in each clinic now? Explain your answer.

   _____

   _____

   _____

Division as Repeated Subtraction

1. Bobby has a box of 24 crayons. He wants to share his crayons equally among as many of his classmates as possible. He decides he will give out 4 crayons to each classmate. Using repeated subtraction, find out how many classmates will each receive 4 crayons.

_____

_____

2. If Bobby decided to give 3 crayons to each classmate, how many students would receive crayons?

_____

3. If Bobby's art class had 12 students, could each student receive crayons from the box of 24? How many would each student receive? _____

4. Four students want to share a total of 16 crayons. They decide to subtract 2 crayons each time to see how many groups of 2 they will make. How many groups of 2 will they make? _____

5. How many crayons will each of the 4 students get? _____

6. **Writing in Math** Brenda and Linda have 12 crayons to share equally. To find out how many crayons each person should get, Brenda decided to make as many groups of 7 crayons as she can. Will Brenda's method work? Explain.

_____

_____

_____

Writing Division Stories

1. Henry wants the same number of apples in each of 5 baskets. Draw a picture of his story and write the division sentence. How many apples will he put in each basket?

_____

2. Bananas are sold 6 to a bunch for small ones and 3 to a bunch for large ones. Robin is buying bananas for her class picnic. There are 24 students in Robin's class. How many bunches of large bananas would she need? How many bunches of small bananas would she need? Write a division sentence for each problem.

_____

_____

3. Darlene and Frank find that a carton of oranges are on sale. Each layer of the carton has 6 oranges and there are 3 layers. If they divided the oranges equally among their 2 brothers and 2 sisters, how many oranges would each receive? Would there be any left over for Darlene and Frank?

_____

4. **Writing in Math** Write your own division story about the number sentence $20 \div 2$.

_____

_____

Name_____

Try, Check, and Revise

In basketball, it is possible to score 1, 2, or 3 points with 1 shot. A regular basket is worth 2 points. A free throw is worth 1 point. A basket from behind the 3-point line is worth 3 points. Hillary scored a total of 10 points in a game. What are two different possibilities for Hillary's scoring if she scored at least two kinds of baskets?

Read and Understand

1. What are the three possible score choices?

_____

2. What are you trying to find?

_____

Plan and Solve

3. Choose one score to try. Divide Hillary's total points by that score.

_____

4. Add another score type, if needed.

_____

5. Solve the problem in a different way.

_____

_____

Look Back and Check

6. Check that both answers equal the same number of points.

_____

_____

Relating Multiplication and Division   PS 7-5

On April 7, 1948, the United Nations created the World Health Organization (WHO). Its goal is to help improve health conditions for all people in the world. The WHO world headquarters is located in Geneva, Switzerland. There are also 6 regional offices throughout the world in Congo, Denmark, India, Washington, D.C., Egypt, and the Philippines.

1. Suppose 12 WHO members from the 6 regional offices have a meeting. Each country sends the same number of people. How many people does each country send? Write a division sentence that solves the problem.

   _____

2. Write a multiplication sentence that uses the same fact family. Explain its meaning.

   _____

   _____

   _____

3. Show how to skip count by 3s to find 18 ÷ 3 = 6.

   _____

4. Show how to skip count by 6s to find 3 × 6 = 18.   _____

The leader of WHO is called the Director-General. Each Director-General can only serve one 5-year term.

5. **Writing in Math** How many Director-Generals would WHO have in a 35-year period? Explain how you could figure out the answer using division and check using multiplication.

   _____

   _____

   _____

Dividing with 2 and 5

Margo is putting new tiles on her kitchen counter.

Here is the 2-tile pattern she uses.

Pattern

1. How many times would each tile be used if Margo used 8 tiles?

   _____

2. If Margo used 4 rows of 8 tiles, how many of each tile would there be?

   _____

3. Margo decided to use a 5-tile pattern. If she used 50 tiles, how many did she use of each type?

   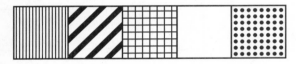

   _____

4. Write the division sentence you used for Exercise 3.

   _____

5. **Writing in Math** During 10 months, a writer wrote 5 children's books. If each book took the same amount of time to write, how long did the writer take to write each book? Explain.

   _____

   _____

   _____

Dividing with 3 and 4

Herbal tea is a very popular drink in the United States. Over 50 years ago, one American woman started a tea company in her home kitchen. The company currently sells thousands of boxes of tea each day. Each type of tea is sold in boxes of 20 tea bags.

1. Cheryl is having a tea party. She will need one box of lemon tea. She places 4 tea bags on each table. How many tables will Cheryl set?

   _____

2. The tea company ships boxes of tea, 12 boxes to a carton. If it wanted the cartons to have 3 layers, draw an array that would describe the carton.

3. The tea company sometimes sells boxes that have several different flavors of tea in the same box. Suppose a box contains 24 tea bags, with equal numbers of mint, orange, and lemon tea bags. How many tea bags of each type are in a box? Show a multiplication sentence that will help you find the answer.

   _____

4. **Writing in Math** Cheryl wants to build shelves to hold her teacup collection. If she has 18 teacups, how many shelves will she need if she wants 3 cups on each shelf? Explain.

   _____

   _____

   _____

Name_____

Dividing with 6 and 7

48 States Alaska and Hawaii are the only 2 states of the United States that do not have a mainland border with the other 48 states. Alaskans sometimes refer to the 48 states as the "lower 48," and people from Hawaii sometimes refer to them as the "mainland."

1. A regional conference of the "lower 48" was held to discuss interstate highway repairs. If 6 regional conferences were held for an equal number of states, how many states were at each conference? _____

2. There are 13 states that were formed from the original colonies. Their representatives met in one meeting room. The rest of the "mainland" states were divided equally into 7 rooms. How many states were represented in each room?

_____

3. When Congress is in session, some representatives stay in Washington, D.C., during the week and travel home on the weekends. Suppose Congress is in session for 42 days in a row, starting on a Monday. If a representative flies home every weekend, how many trips home will she take? _____

4. A representative tells her staff they must work every weekday while in session. How many days must they work?

_____

5. **Writing in Math** A group of 36 people toured the United Nations in New York. There were 6 tour guides available to show them around. An equal number of people went into each group. Draw a picture to show how many people were with each tour guide.

Dividing with 8 and 9

An array of 64 small squares are arranged to
form one large square.

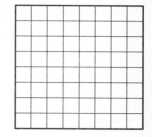

1. How many squares are on each side?

   _____

2. Complete the pattern by coloring every other small
   square, as shown in the picture. How many small
   squares are colored in?

   _____

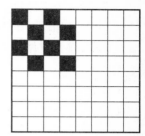

3. Look at the design at the right. If 81 small-sized
   triangles fit inside the big triangle, how many would fit
   in each of the 9 medium-sized triangles? Write the
   division sentence.

   _____

4. If you shaded in the 27 triangles at the 3 corners, how
   many small-sized triangles would be shaded in each
   corner? Find the division answer through a multiplication
   question.

   _____

5. **Writing in Math** Medium-sized triangles are being sold
   3 for $6.00. You have $54 to spend. How many big
   triangles can you make if you spend all of your money?
   Explain your answer.

   _____

   _____

   _____

   _____

Name_____

Dividing with 0 and 1

Lorne, Todd, and Scott worked for a delivery service. Every weekday they picked up packages from location A and took them across town to location B. Here was the work schedule for last week.

Monday	8 packages
Tuesday	4 packages
Wednesday	6 packages
Thursday	3 packages
Friday	0 packages

1. On Monday, Todd and Scott were the drivers on duty. If each one took an equal amount of packages, how many would each deliver to location B?

   _____

2. On Tuesday, Lorne was the only driver. Show a division sentence that explains how many packages Lorne delivered to location B.

   _____

3. On Thursday, all the packages went to the same person, so they were packed in a single carton. Write a division sentence that shows how many packages were in the 1 carton.

   _____

4. Write a division sentence to show how many cartons were packed on Thursday if 3 packages fit into each carton.

   _____

5. **Writing in Math** Todd, Lorne, and Scott showed up for work on Friday. Each person was going to deliver the same number of packages. But there had been a terrible snowstorm that day, so there were no packages to deliver. Write a division sentence to show how many packages each one delivered. Explain your answer.

   _____

   _____

   _____

Remainders

Ms. Leonard has organized her math class so that she completes a unit every 7 days, including homework for weekends. In months that are longer than 28 days, the extra days are for math activities, such as math games, math puzzles, and reading about famous people in math history.

1. This is a leap year, so February has 29 days. How many units will she complete? How many days will be left for math activities?

   _____

2. September has 30 days but the first 2 days of the month are during summer vacation. Will the students have time for math activities in September? _____

3. November has 31 days. How many days will the students have for math activities? _____

Students are making bows to decorate the school assembly. Mr. Carson's class has designed a small bow that will take 5 in. of ribbon to make and a large bow that will take 9 in. of ribbon to make. Ribbon is on sale for 3 yd for $1. (Hint: There are 36 in. in a yard.)

4. How many small bows can they make from 1 yd of ribbon? _____

5. How much ribbon will be left over? _____

6. Mr. Carson told them that they must make at least 2 large bows. How many small bows can they make? How much ribbon will be left over? Explain how you solved the problem.

   _____

   _____

   _____

Name_____

Division Patterns with 10, 11, 12

A decade is 10 years long. In 1817, James Monroe became the 5th president of the United States, and 40 years later, James Buchanan became the 15th president of the United States.

1. How many decades passed between Monroe and Buchanan?

   _____

2. President Theodore Roosevelt was 60 years old at the time of his death. How many decades did Theodore Roosevelt live?

   _____

3. John Quincy Adams, the 2nd president, lived for 90 years. For how many decades did John Quincy Adams live?

   _____

4. Andrew planted a tree in his backyard. The tree grew 11 in. each year. If the tree is now 66 in. tall, how many years ago did Andrew plant it?

   _____

5. **Writing in Math** Esther needed 72 eggs for the football team breakfast. How many dozen eggs does she need? Explain.

   _____

   _____

   _____

   _____

PROBLEM-SOLVING SKILL

Translating Words to Expressions

Each key on a piano plays a note that is different from any other note on the piano. If you play a C and then play the next 6 white keys on the piano, you will play all the notes in a "major scale." It sounds like the do-re-mi notes you might know.

Piano Keyboard

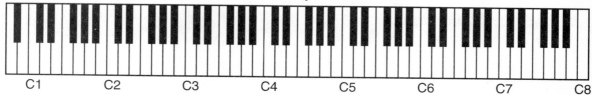

C1 C2 C3 C4 C5 C6 C7 C8

1. If you played 28 white keys in a row starting at the C1 key, write a numerical expression for how many major scales you would have played. _____

2. If you played a total of 49 white keys, starting with C2, write a numerical expression for how many major scales you would have played. _____

3. There are 2 fewer black keys than the 7 white keys between one C note and the next. Write an expression for the number of black keys between C6 and C7. _____

4. Starting after C4, there are 4 sets of white and 4 sets of black keys on the right side of the piano. Write an expression for those keys. _____

5. **Writing in Math** The following numerical expressions could describe the piano's 88 keys. The white keys = $2 + (7 \times 7) + 1$. The black keys = $1 + (7 \times 5)$. Write the expressions in words.

_____

_____

_____

_____

Name_____

Numerical Expressions

Susan's mom said that she could write four different math problems using the numbers 4, 3, and 2 in this reverse order that would result in the answers 1, 2, 3, and 4. Only addition and subtraction can be used, not all need to be used, and a number may be used more than once.

Read and Understand

1. What is the order of the numbers for
   each problem?   _____

2. What are the answers being created?

   _____

Plan and Solve

3. What operations can you use
   for each problem?   _____

4. What strategy would you use?

   _____

5. Write the four numerical expressions with their answers.

   _____

   _____

Look Back and Check

6. Explain how you can check your answer.

   _____

   _____

Solid Figures

You can find shapes everywhere in the world around you. Every object has a shape. Some are easy to describe, while others are combinations of two or more shapes.

Baseball   **Party hat**

Toy box

1. The baseball is what kind of solid figure? Does the baseball have any flat surfaces? _____

2. The party hat is what kind of solid figure? Give an example of another object like this.

   _____

3. The toy box is what kind of a solid figure? Name another object that has this shape. Does the toy box have any flat surfaces?

   _____

4. The object shown in the drawing is what kind of a solid figure?

   _____

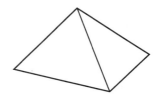

5. The letter block is what kind of solid figure?

   _____

6. **Writing in Math** Could you carve a cone out of a cylinder? Explain.

   _____

   _____

Relating Solids and Shapes

Many buildings and homes use smokestacks.
A smokestack is especially important for a
home fireplace. Some ashes float away from
the fire and are moved outside through the
chimney.

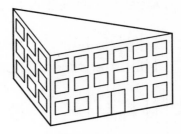

1. What kind of solid figure is the
smokestack?

_____

2. How many edges does it have?   _____

3. How many corners does it have?   _____

Sometimes people build buildings with unusual
shapes. The drawing shows a building in
the shape of a wedge.

4. How many corners does it have?

_____

5. Find a rectangular face. How many
corners does the rectangular face have?   _____

6. How many edges are on each
rectangular face?   _____

7. Writing in Math Explain why a cube has the same number
of corners as a rectangular prism.

_____

_____

_____

_____

PROBLEM-SOLVING STRATEGY
Act It Out

Gifts A gift store had a special sale. If you bought 3 gifts, you would get 1 for free. If Sarah bought 9 gifts, how many gifts did she get for free?

Read and Understand

1. How many gifts do you have to buy to get 1 for free? _____

2. How many gifts did Sarah buy? _____

3. What are you trying to find?

_____

Plan and Solve

4. What strategy will you use? _____

5. What objects do you need to act it out? _____

6. Solve the problem, and write your answer in a complete sentence.

_____

_____

Look Back and Check

7. Is your answer reasonable?

_____

Solve Another Problem

8. Billy plays baseball. For every 5 hits he gets he strikes out 1 time. If Billy strikes out 5 times, how many hits does he get? _____

Name_____

Lines and Line Segments

1. What is an exact position called?   _____

2. What is a set of points that is endless in
   both directions called?   _____

3. What is part of a line called?   _____

4. What is part of a line that is endless in
   one direction called?   _____

5. How could you change a line into a line segment?

   _____

   _____

6. How could you change a line segment into a ray?

   _____

7. Are the lines shown intersecting lines or
   parallel lines?

   _____

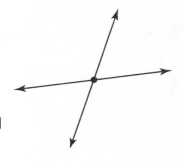

8. **Writing in Math** Draw two rays that are not parallel
   to each other and never intersect. Explain.

   _____

   _____

   _____

Angles

The most famous tower in the world is probably the
Eiffel Tower in Paris, France. It is full of angles.
Tell whether each angle below, all of which can
be found in the lower part of the Eiffel Tower,
is right, acute, or obtuse.

   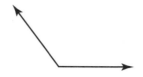

1. _____ **2.** _____ **3.** _____

On the three clocks, draw an acute, a right, and an obtuse angle
with the hour and minute hands. Then tell what time you drew.

4. _____ **5.** _____ **6.** _____

7. **Writing in Math** Amy said that two perpendicular lines
   create four right angles. Is she correct? Explain.

_____

_____

_____

_____

_____

_____

Polygons

You can draw lines connecting the angles of a polygon to make new polygons. Follow the directions for 1–5.

1. Draw a line connecting two angles of the hexagon to make a triangle and a pentagon.

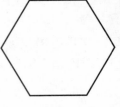

2. Draw a line connecting two angles of the hexagon to make two quadrilaterals.

3. Draw two lines connecting angles of the hexagon to make a quadrilateral and two triangles.

4. Draw two lines connecting angles of the hexagon to make four quadrilaterals.

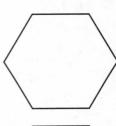

5. Draw three lines connecting angles of the hexagon to make six triangles.

6. Writing in Math A hexagon has one more side than a pentagon. Does that mean you could not draw a hexagon inside a pentagon? Explain.

_____

_____

_____

_____

Triangles

Use what you know about triangles to complete Exercises 1–5.
Read each statement. Write whether the statement is true or
false. If the statement is false, write a true statement.

1. A right triangle has three right angles.

_____

_____

2. A triangle that has three sides of the same length is an isosceles triangle.

_____

_____

3. An obtuse triangle has two angles that are acute.

_____

_____

4. In a right triangle, the two angles that are not right angles
are acute.

_____

_____

5. A scalene triangle cannot be an acute triangle.

_____

_____

6. Writing in Math Do you think it is easier to draw a
equilateral triangle or a scalene triangle? Explain.

_____

_____

© Pearson Education, Inc. 3

Use with Lesson 8-7. **103**

Name_____

Quadrilaterals

Write the name of the quadrilateral that is being described. Be careful! Some may have more than one correct answer. If this is so, write all correct answers.

1. I have four sides and all of my sides have the same length. What am I?

    _____

2. I have four sides. My opposite sides are parallel and equal in length. Each angle is a right angle. What am I?

    _____

3. I have four sides. My opposite sides are parallel and equal in length. My four sides are not all equal in length. What am I?

    _____

4. I have only one pair of parallel sides. What am I?

    _____

5. You can make my shape by using exactly two triangles. What am I?

    _____

6. **Writing in Math** Amanda said that a square and a rhombus are the same, except that a square has all right angles. Is she correct? Explain.

    _____

    _____

    _____

    _____

Congruent Figures and Motion

Tell whether you would slide, turn, or flip the first figure to get the second figure.

1.

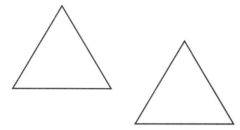

_____

2.

_____

3.

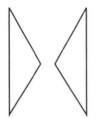

_____

4.

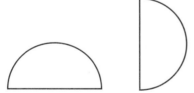

_____

5.

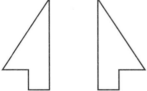

_____

6. Writing in Math Look at the figures for Exercise 5. Are they congruent? Explain.

_____

_____

Symmetry

1. Is the guitar symmetric? If it is, how many lines of symmetry does it have?

_____

2. Is the baseball bat symmetric? If it is, how many lines of symmetry does it have?

_____

3. Is the fork symmetric? If it is, how many lines of symmetry does it have?

_____

4. Does a circle have more than one line of symmetry? Explain.

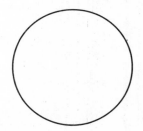

_____

_____

5. **Writing in Math** Which numeral from 5 to 9 is symmetric? Explain your answer.

_____

_____

Perimeter

Many sports are played on fields or courts. These form
geometric figures.

1. A football field forms a rectangle.
   Look at the drawing. Find the
   perimeter.

   _____

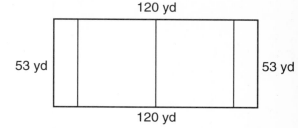

2. The infield of a professional
   baseball diamond forms a
   square. Look at the drawing.
   Find the perimeter.

   _____

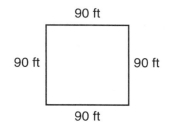

3. A bowling lane forms a rectangle.
   Look at the drawing. Find the
   perimeter.

   _____

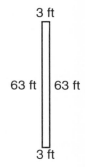

4. A tennis court forms a rectangle.
   Look at the drawing. Find the
   perimeter.

   _____

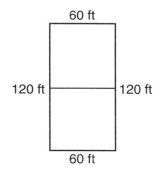

5. **Writing in Math** If you know the length of one side of a
   square, can you find its perimeter? Explain.

   _____

   _____

   _____

Name_____

Area

At the zoo there are special places for all kinds of different animals.

1. The drawing shows a special cage for one Bengal tiger. What is the area of the cage in square units?

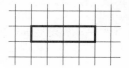

_____

2. The drawing shows the tiger area in a zoo. What is its area in square units?

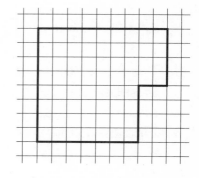

_____

3. What is the area, in square units, of the indoor gorilla space shown in the drawing?

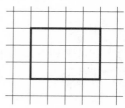

_____

4. What is the area, in square units, of the outdoor gorilla space shown in the drawing?

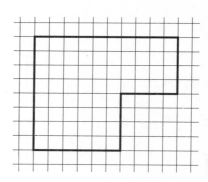

_____

5. **Writing in Math** Roy says that a figure that has an area of 1 square unit will have a perimeter of 1 unit. Is he correct? Explain.

_____

_____

_____

Volume

Swimming pools hold a lot of water. Use what you know about finding volume for 1–4. If you want to, use cubes to build a model.

1. Find the volume of a pool that is 5 cubes long, 3 cubes wide, and 2 cubes deep. Write your answer in cubic units.

    _____

2. Find the volume of a pool that is 4 cubes long, 2 cubes wide, and 2 cubes deep. Write your answer in cubic units.

    _____

3. Suppose you have a pool that holds 36 cubic units of water. The width is 3 cubes, and the pool is 3 cubes deep. How many cubes long is the pool?

    _____

4. Suppose you have a pool that holds 45 cubic units of water. The pool is 5 cubes long and 3 cubes wide. How many cubes deep is your pool?

    _____

5. **Writing in Math** Look at the model for a pool that has a deep end and a shallow end. The model is shown upside down so you can see the cubes better. How many cubic units of water does it hold? Explain how you found your answer.

    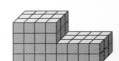

    _____

    _____

    _____

    _____

Name_____

Writing to Describe

Look at the two triangles. Use geometric
terms to describe how they are alike.

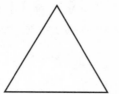

> **Read and Understand**

1. What are you trying to find?

_____

> **Plan and Solve**

2. Write geometric terms that tell about the triangles.

_____

3. Write the geometric terms that describe
   how they are alike.   _____

4. Write your answer in a complete sentence using geometric terms.

_____

> **Look Back and Check**

5. Is your answer reasonable? Explain.

_____

_____

_____

Solve Another Problem

6. Look at the two figures. Use geometric
   terms to describe how they are alike.

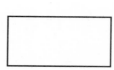

_____

_____

Name_____

PROBLEM-SOLVING APPLICATION

Pyramid

Look at the drawing of a pyramid. How many cubes are needed to make the pyramid?

Read and Understand

1. What do you know?

_____

_____

2. What are you trying to find?

_____

_____

Plan and Solve

3. What objects do you need to act out the problem? _____

4. Solve the problem, and write your answer in a complete sentence.

_____

Look Back and Check

5. Is your answer reasonable?

_____

Solve Another Problem

6. Look at the drawing of a rectangular prism. How many cubes are needed to make the solid figure?

_____

Equal Parts of a Whole

Jenny's mom baked three loaves of bread. She cut the first loaf into 6 equal pieces, the second into 8 equal pieces, and the third loaf into 10 equal pieces.

1. Name the equal parts of the first loaf of bread.

   _____

2. Name the equal parts of the second loaf of bread.

   _____

3. Name the equal parts of the third loaf of bread.

   _____

4. Do the shelves in Bookcase A divide the bookcase into equal parts? If so, name the equal parts.

   _____

5. Do the shelves in Bookcase B divide the bookcase into equal parts? If so, name the equal parts.

   _____

Bookcase A   **Bookcase B**

6. **Writing in Math** Which has larger parts, a four-inch square divided into fifths or a four-inch square divided into sixths? Explain.

   _____

   _____

   _____

   _____

   _____

   _____

Naming Fractional Parts

1. What fraction of the circle is shaded?

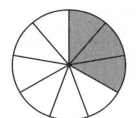

_____

2. What fraction of the circle is not shaded?

_____

3. What fraction of boxes in the rectangle are numbered 1?

1	3	3	3	2
4	3	1	1	2

_____

4. What fraction of boxes in the rectangle are numbered 2? _____

5. What fraction of boxes in the rectangle are numbered 3? _____

6. What fraction of boxes in the rectangle are numbered 4? _____

7. What fraction of the triangle is shaded?

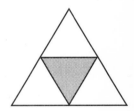

_____

8. What fraction of the triangle is not shaded?

_____

9. Writing in Math Which fraction of the triangle is larger, the shaded part or the part that is not shaded? Explain.

_____

_____

_____

_____

Name_____

Equivalent Fractions

Continue each pattern.

1. $\dfrac{1}{4} = \dfrac{2}{8} = \dfrac{3}{12} = \dfrac{4}{\boxed{}} = \dfrac{5}{\boxed{}} = \dfrac{6}{\boxed{}}$

2. $\dfrac{2}{5} = \dfrac{4}{10} = \dfrac{6}{15} = \dfrac{\boxed{}}{20} = \dfrac{\boxed{}}{25} = \dfrac{\boxed{}}{30}$

3. $\dfrac{1}{3} = \dfrac{2}{6} = \dfrac{3}{9} = \dfrac{4}{\boxed{}} = \dfrac{\boxed{}}{15} = \dfrac{6}{\boxed{}}$

4. Shade each picture to match the number sentence.

$\dfrac{1}{2} = \dfrac{4}{8}$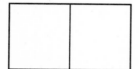

5. Angie gave away 2 pieces of her orange. How many pieces would Gary need to give away to equal the pieces of orange Angie gave away?

_____

6. Writing in Math Can a fraction with a 2 in the numerator equal $\dfrac{1}{2}$? Explain. You may use fraction strips to help.

_____

_____

_____

_____

_____

Comparing and Ordering Fractions

1. During which month did it rain the most?

_____

2. Did it rain more in March or July?

_____

3. During which month did it rain the least?

_____

Rainfall	
March	$\frac{7}{10}$ in.
April	$\frac{1}{5}$ in.
May	$\frac{1}{2}$ in.
June	$\frac{9}{10}$ in.
July	$\frac{4}{5}$ in.

4. Which month had the lower rainfall, May or March?   _____

5. During which months was rainfall more than $\frac{1}{2}$ in.?

_____

6. During which months was rainfall less than $\frac{1}{3}$ in.?   _____

7. During which months was rainfall more than $\frac{3}{5}$ in.?

_____

8. Order the months from least to greatest rainfall.

_____

9. Writing in Math One-quarter of the students in Mr. Garcia's class ride the bus to school and $\frac{5}{8}$ walk to school. Do more students walk or ride the bus? Explain.

_____

_____

_____

_____

Name_____

Estimating Fractional Amounts

Shade a Fraction Draw and shade each figure.

1. A square with about $\frac{1}{3}$ shaded

2. A circle with about $\frac{5}{6}$ shaded

3. A rectangle with about $\frac{2}{5}$ shaded

4. A square with about $\frac{5}{8}$ shaded

5. **Writing in Math** About what fraction of the figure is shaded? How can you tell? Explain.

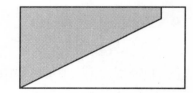

_____

_____

_____

_____

Fractions on the Number Line

Write each fraction on the number line.

1. $\frac{3}{6}$

2. $\frac{5}{6}$

3. $\frac{1}{6}$

4. $\frac{4}{6}$

5. $\frac{2}{6}$

6. What fraction does each mark on the number line represent? _____

7. Write the fractions in order from greatest to least.

_____

8. Write three fractions you could plot between $\frac{1}{8}$ and $\frac{1}{2}$ on the number line.

_____

9. **Writing in Math** How can you use a number line to tell if a fraction is less than $\frac{1}{2}$? Explain.

_____

_____

_____

Name_____

Fractions and Sets

Draw a picture to show each fraction of a set.

1. $\frac{1}{4}$ of the animals are dogs.

2. $\frac{2}{3}$ of the shapes are circles.

3. $\frac{3}{4}$ of the windows in the house are open.

4. $\frac{7}{8}$ of the shapes are stars.

5. **Writing in Math** For Exercise 2, explain how you could show that $\frac{2}{3}$ of the shapes are circles if there were 6 shapes in all.

_____

_____

_____

Finding Fractional Parts of a Set

Crayons The box of crayons has 24 crayons.

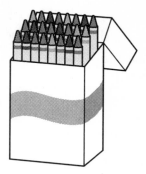

1. Samara colored with $\frac{1}{4}$ of the crayons.
   How many crayons did she color with?

   _____

2. Max lost $\frac{1}{2}$ of the crayons. How many
   crayons did he lose?   _____

3. Tamika broke $\frac{1}{8}$ of the crayons. How many
   crayons did she break?   _____

4. Pedro used 10 crayons in art class. Did he
   use more than or less than $\frac{1}{2}$ of the crayons? _____

5. Mrs. Kim gave $\frac{1}{12}$ of the crayons to Debbie.
   How many crayons did she give to Debbie?   _____

6. During art class, $\frac{1}{3}$ of the crayons fell out of the
   box. How many crayons fell out of the box?   _____

7. If you divide the crayons into 4 equal groups,
   how many crayons will be in each group?   _____

8. **Writing in Math** Ben used 9 of the crayons to make a
   birthday card for his friend. Did he use more than or less
   than $\frac{1}{3}$ of the crayons? Explain.

   _____

   _____

   _____

   _____

Name_____

Adding and Subtracting Fractions

Jim's Neighborhood The chart shows the distances between some places in Jim's neighborhood.

From	To	Distance
Jim's house	Library	$\frac{2}{8}$ miles
Library	Bank	$\frac{5}{8}$ miles
Jim's house	School	$\frac{4}{8}$ miles
School	Library	$\frac{1}{8}$ miles
Jim's house	Grocery store	$\frac{3}{8}$ miles
Grocery store	Bank	$\frac{3}{8}$ miles

1. Jim walked from his house to school. After school, he walked to the library. How far did he walk? _____

2. From Jim's house, how much farther is it to the grocery store than to the library? _____

3. Jim walked from his house to the library. Then he walked from the library to the bank. How far did he walk? _____

4. From Jim's house, how much farther is it to the school than to the library? _____

5. Jim rode his bike from his house to the grocery store. Then he rode to the bank. How far did he ride? _____

6. From Jim's house, how much farther is it to the school than to the grocery store? _____

7. **Writing in Math** On Friday, Jim walked to the library and back home. On Saturday, he walked to the grocery store and back home. On which day did he walk farther? Explain.

_____

_____

_____

Mixed Numbers

Vacations Debbie, Ross, and Bridget each went on vacation with their family over the summer. They all spent a different amount of time on vacation. (Remember: There are 7 days in 1 week.)

1. Debbie's family went on vacation for $1\frac{2}{7}$ weeks. How many days is that?

   _____

2. Ross's family went on vacation for $2\frac{1}{7}$ weeks. How many days is that?

   _____

3. Bridget's family went on vacation for $2\frac{6}{7}$ weeks. How many days is that?

   _____

Shade each picture to match the mixed number.

4. $1\frac{3}{4}$

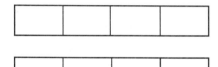

5. $3\frac{1}{2}$

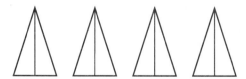

6. **Writing in Math** Keri shaded $5\frac{2}{3}$ circles. Did she shade more than or less than 6 whole circles? Explain.

   _____

   _____

   _____

Name_____

Solve a Simpler Problem

Birdhouse Andy was cutting wood to make a birdhouse. He cut a board into 4 pieces. Then he cut each piece in half. He used 6 of the pieces. How many pieces were left?

Read and Understand

1. How many pieces did Andy cut the board into at first?   _____

2. How did Andy cut the pieces after that?

_____

3. How many pieces of wood did he use?   _____

4. What are you trying to find?

_____

Plan and Solve

5. How many pieces of wood did Andy have after both cuts?   _____

6. Solve the problem. Write your answer in a complete sentence.

_____

Look Back and Check

7. Explain how you can check your answer.

_____

Solve Another Problem

8. Tariq made 26 muffins for the bake sale. He sold 20 muffins. He divided the leftover muffins equally between 2 friends. How many muffins did each friend get?   _____

Length

Measure the perimeter of each figure to the nearest inch.

1.

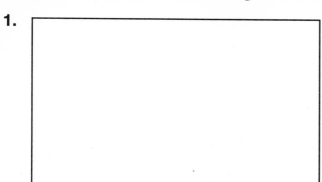

2.

3.

4.

5. Writing in Math Explain how you found the perimeter of the rectangle in Exercise 4.

_____

_____

Measuring to the Nearest $\frac{1}{2}$ and $\frac{1}{4}$ Inch

Line A _____

Line B _____

Line C _____

1. Measure the length of line *A* to the nearest $\frac{1}{4}$ inch. _____

2. Measure the length of line *B* to the nearest $\frac{1}{4}$ inch. _____

3. Measure the length of line *C* to the nearest $\frac{1}{2}$ inch. _____

4. Measure the length of line *B* to the nearest $\frac{1}{2}$ inch. _____

5. Draw a square that is $1\frac{1}{4}$ inches long.

6. **Writing in Math** Explain why a measurement to the nearest $\frac{1}{4}$ inch could be 3 in. even though 3 is a whole number.

_____

_____

_____

_____

_____

_____

Name_____

Length in Feet and Inches

Use the table to find the height of each person in inches.

Evan	4 feet, 6 inches
Nadia	5 feet, 1 inch
Lucas	4 feet, 10 inches
Serena	4 feet, 8 inches

1. Lucas   _____

2. Evan   _____

3. Serena   _____

4. Nadia   _____

5. Marnie, Andrew, and Sara each planted a pine tree in their neighborhood park. After one year, they measured their trees. Marnie's tree was 33 inches tall, Andrew's tree was 3 feet tall, and Sara's tree was 3 feet, 4 inches tall. List the tree heights in order from greatest to least.

_____

6. Female polar bears grow to about 6 feet long. How many inches is that?   _____

7. A Komodo dragon can grow to be 9 feet long. How many inches is that?   _____

8. A stick insect can grow up to 15 inches long. How long is that in feet and inches?   _____

9. **Writing in Math** Which measurement is longer, 25 inches or 2 feet, 4 inches? Explain.

_____

_____

Feet, Yards, and Miles

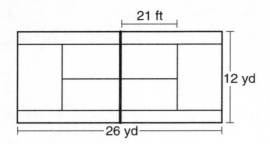

1. The width of a tennis court is 12 yd. How many feet is that?   _____

2. How wide is a tennis court in inches?   _____

3. The length of a tennis court is 26 yd. How many feet is that?   _____

4. The length of a rectangle that a tennis player can hit a serve into is 21 ft. How many inches is that?   _____

5. Complete the table.

Yards	1	2	3	4	5	6	7	8
Feet	3	6	9	12	15		21	

6. **Writing in Math** Would you measure the length of your front yard in yards, feet, or inches? Explain.

_____

_____

_____

_____

_____

_____

PROBLEM-SOLVING SKILL

Extra or Missing Information

In Mr. Thompson's class, $\frac{1}{8}$ of the students have pet cats. How many students have pet cats? Decide if the problem has extra or missing information. Solve if you have enough information.

Read and Understand

1. What fraction of the students in Mr. Thompson's class have pet cats?   _____

2. What are you trying to find?

   _____

Plan and Solve

3. Do you have enough information to solve the problem? If so, how many students have pet cats?   _____

4. If you do not have enough information, what would you need to know to solve the problem?

   _____

   _____

Look Back and Check

5. Explain how you can check your answer.

   _____

Solve Another Problem

6. The table shows how far each person ran in one week. How far did Kirby, Jorge, and Anna run altogether? If there is not enough information to solve the problem, tell what information you need.

Name	Distance Run
Kirby	12 mi
Jorge	15 mi
Anna	17 mi

Name_____

Orange Slices

Arman divided an orange into 8 equal slices. Then he cut each slice in half. He ate 12 slices. How many slices were left?

Read and Understand

1. How many slices did Arman have after he divided the orange the first time? _____

2. How did Arman cut the slices after that?

_____

3. How many slices of orange did he eat? _____

4. What are you trying to find?

_____

Plan and Solve

5. How many slices of orange did Arman have after he cut each slice in half? _____

6. Solve the problem. Write your answer in a complete sentence.

_____

Look Back and Check

7. Explain how you can check your answer.

_____

Solve Another Problem

8. Sergio had 18 marbles. He got 12 more marbles for his birthday. Then he gave 16 marbles to Pamela. How many marbles did he have left? _____

Name_____

Tenths

Ice Skating Out of 10 friends who went ice skating, 7 of the friends had their own skates and 3 had to rent skates.

1. Write a fraction and a decimal to show the number of friends who had their own skates. _____

2. Write a fraction and a decimal to show the number of friends who rented skates. _____

Biking The chart shows how many miles each person biked. Write a decimal to show how many miles each person biked.

Name	Miles Biked
Sonia	$3\frac{4}{10}$
Peter	$6\frac{8}{10}$
Venus	$2\frac{5}{10}$
Gabriel	$1\frac{3}{10}$
Monica	$4\frac{1}{10}$
Jeff	$5\frac{9}{10}$

3. Venus _____

4. Jeff _____

5. Monica _____

6. Peter _____

7. Sonia _____

8. Gabriel _____

9. **Writing in Math** Yvette's mother asked Yvette to give her one tenth of the watermelon. Explain how Yvette could do this.

_____

_____

_____

_____

Name_____

Hundredths

CD Collection Sachi has 100 CDs. The chart shows how many she has of each type. Write a fraction and a decimal to show what part of her CD collection is each type of music.

1. Country _____

2. Rock _____

3. Reggae _____

4. Classical _____

Sachi's CD Collection

Classical	7
Rock	56
Country	23
Reggae	14

Paint Colors Hanson is an artist. He keeps his paint tubes in a large case. The chart shows how many shades of each color are in the case. Write a fraction and a decimal to show what part of his paints are shades of each color.

Color	Number of Tubes
Red	21
Orange	4
Yellow	6
Green	16
Blue	27
Purple	11
Brown	15

5. Blue _____

6. Red _____

7. Green _____

8. Yellow _____ **9.** Brown _____

10. Orange _____ **11.** Purple _____

12. Writing in Math Explain how you could use a hundredths grid to show how 7 hundredths is different from 7 tenths.

_____

_____

_____

_____

© Pearson Education, Inc. 2

Name_____

Comparing and Ordering Decimals   PS 10-3

Tiny Animals The chart shows the lengths of some of the world's smallest animals.

Tiny Animals

Type of Animal	Length (in.)
Dwarf goby fish	0.30
Jaragua lizard	0.63
Fairy fly	0.01
Brazilian frog	0.33

1. Which is smaller, the fairy fly or the dwarf goby fish?

   _____

2. Which is larger, the Brazilian frog or the Jaragua lizard?

   _____

3. Which is smaller, the Brazilian frog or the dwarf goby fish?

   _____

4. Which is larger, the fairy fly or the Jaragua lizard?

   _____

Salad Tony is making a salad. The chart shows how many pounds of each vegetable he bought at the grocery store.

Vegetable	Weight (lb)
Tomato	1.45
Cucumber	1.09
Carrot	1.73

1.00 1.10 1.20 1.30 1.40 1.50 1.60 1.70 1.80 1.90 2.00

5. Order the weight of the vegetables from greatest to least. Use the number line to help.

   _____

6. **Writing in Math** Explain how you could write 0.7 differently to make it easier to compare 0.7 and 0.73.

   _____

   _____

Adding and Subtracting Decimals   PS 10-4

Exercise Phoebe likes to take long walks. The chart shows how far she walked each day.

Day	Distance (in mi)
Monday	2.24
Tuesday	1.78
Wednesday	1.33
Thursday	2.02
Friday	0.96

1. How far did Phoebe walk on Monday and Wednesday combined?

   _____

2. How much farther did Phoebe walk on Thursday than on Tuesday?

   _____

3. How far did Phoebe walk on Tuesday and Friday combined?   _____

4. How much farther did Phoebe walk on Wednesday than on Friday?   _____

5. If Omar walked 2.14 mi on Tuesday, how much farther did he walk than Phoebe on Tuesday?   _____

6. How far did Phoebe walk on Tuesday and Thursday combined?   _____

7. On which two days did Phoebe walk a total of 2.98 mi?

   _____

8. **Writing in Math** Which is farther, the distance Phoebe walked on Monday and Wednesday combined or the distance she walked on Tuesday and Thursday combined? Explain.

   _____

   _____

   _____

PROBLEM-SOLVING STRATEGY

Make an Organized List

Getting Dressed Jackie is deciding what to wear. She needs to choose one top and one bottom. How many different outfits can she wear?

Tops	Bottoms
T-shirt	Pants
Sweater	Shorts
Blouse	Skirt

Read and Understand

1. How many tops and bottoms can she choose from?

   _____

2. What are you trying to find?

   _____

   _____

Plan and Solve

3. Make a list of all the possible outfits.

   _____

   _____

   _____

   _____

4. How many different outfits can she wear? Write your answer in a complete sentence.

   _____

   _____

Look Back and Check

5. Explain how you can check your answer.

   _____

   _____

Centimeters and Decimeters

Measure the perimeter of each figure to the nearest centimeter.

1.

_____

2.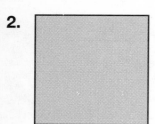

_____

3. Draw a line that is 1 dm long.

4. Draw a square with a perimeter of 16 cm.

5. Writing in Math Would it be better to measure the length of your desk in centimeters or decimeters? Explain.

_____

_____

_____

Name_____

Meters and Kilometers

Driving The chart shows the
distances between some cities
in Massachusetts.

To	From	Distance (in km)
Boston	Lowell	50
Lowell	Brockton	80
Brockton	Plymouth	67
Plymouth	Falmouth	56

1. Henry drove from Boston to Lowell.
   Then he drove from Lowell to Brockton.
   Which distance was greater? How much
   greater?

   _____

2. Allison drove from Lowell to Brockton. Then she drove from
   Brockton to Plymouth. Which distance was greater? How
   much greater?

   _____

3. Kirk drove from Brockton to Plymouth. Then he drove from
   Plymouth to Falmouth. Which distance was greater? How
   much greater?

   _____

4. A ceiling is 4 m high. What is the height
   in centimeters?   _____

5. It is 2 km from Ursala's house to school.
   What is the distance in meters?   _____

6. **Writing in Math** Greg said that since there are 100 cm in a
   meter and 10 cm in a decimeter, there must be 10 dm in a
   meter. Is he correct? Explain.

   _____

   _____

   _____

Name_____

Writing to Explain

Tables and Chairs Kyle and Becky are setting up tables and chairs for a party. Complete the table. Then explain how the number of chairs changes as the number of tables changes.

Number of tables	1	2	3	4	5
Number of chairs	4	8	12		

Read and Understand

1. How many chairs are used for one table? Two tables? Three tables?

_____

2. What are you trying to find?

_____

Plan and Solve

3. Complete the table.

4. Explain how the number of chairs changes as the number of tables changes.

_____

_____

_____

Look Back and Check

5. Explain how you can check your answer.

_____

_____

Name_____

Lunch Choices

You can have one juice choice and one food choice for lunch. How many different lunches can you choose?

Juice	Food
Apple juice	Sandwich
Orange juice	Burrito

Read and Understand

1. How many juice choices do you have?   _____

2. How many food choices do you have?   _____

3. What are you trying to find?

   _____

Plan and Solve

4. What strategy can you use to solve the problem?

   _____

5. Make a list of all the possible lunches.

   _____

   _____

6. How many different lunches can you choose? Write your answer in a complete sentence.

   _____

Look Back and Check

7. Explain how you can check your answer.

   _____

   _____

Name_____

Mental Math: Multiplication Patterns

Coins are often distributed in rolls. Coins are counted and put into a paper tube. Each tube then has a value, determined by the number and type of coin it holds.

1. If a roll of dimes is worth 500 cents, how much are 3 rolls of dimes worth?

   _____

2. If a roll of pennies is worth 50 cents, how much are 7 rolls of pennies worth?

   _____

3. If a roll of nickels is worth 200 cents, how much are 4 rolls of nickels worth?

   _____

4. If a roll of quarters is worth 1,000 cents, how much are 9 rolls of quarters worth?

   _____

5. **Writing in Math** There are 40 quarters in a roll, and 1 roll of quarters is worth 1,000 cents. Merle is 3 quarters short of having 6 rolls of quarters. Explain how you can use mental math to find how much money Merle has in cents.

   _____

   _____

   _____

   _____

   _____

Estimating Products

1. Kim lives 230 mi from her grandmother. If Kim drives 59 mi per hour, will she be able to reach her grandmother's house in less than 5 hr?

_____

2. Pencils cost $0.08 each. Margo wants to buy one pencil for each of the students in her class. There are 31 students in Margo's class. Margo has $2.50. Will she have enough money to buy the pencils?

_____

3. Chez is decorating her school bulletin board with photographs from the school holiday party. The bulletin board is divided into 18 sections, and each section can hold 9 photos. About how many photos can Chez put on the bulletin board?

_____

4. Cheryl wants to know how many marbles it will take to fill a glass jar. She knows that the jar has a volume of 42 cubic inches. She found that she can put 8 marbles into 1 cubic inch. About how many marbles will it take to fill the jar?

_____

5. **Writing in Math** Sanchez says the best estimate for 9×86 is 720. Sandy says the best estimate is 810. Who is correct? Explain.

_____

_____

_____

_____

Mental Math: Division Patterns

At a festival, firefighters set up a booth to make children aware of fire safety. The firefighters handed out buttons.

Firefighter	Number of Buttons
Frank	600
Jacob	360
Janet	4,800
Ken	3,000
Sylvia	400

1. Janet worked in the booth all 6 days of the festival. On average, how many buttons did she hand out each day?

   _____

2. Frank worked in the booth 3 days. On average, how many buttons did he hand out each day?

   _____

3. Sylvia worked in the booth 4 days of the festival. On average, how many buttons did she hand out each day?

   _____

4. **Writing in Math** Janet worked in the booth for 8 hr each day. Use your answer to Exercise 1 to find how many buttons Janet passed out each hour on average. Explain.

   _____

   _____

   _____

   _____

Estimating Quotients

A pet shelter keeps kittens where people can see and play with them. Last week 26 cat toys were donated to the shelter to divide among the kittens.

1. About how many toys can each kitten have if there are 6 kittens in the shelter?

   _____

2. If each kitten receives 3 toys, about how many kittens are there in the shelter?

   _____

3. A worker decided that since there are only 4 kittens in the shelter right now, she would store half of the toys and give the other half of the toys to the kittens. About how many toys will each of the 4 kittens have to play with?

   _____

4. If there were 10 kittens in the shelter and each already had 1 toy, about how many toys will each have after the 26 new toys are passed out?

   _____

5. **Writing in Math** A small box of raisins has about 37 raisins in it. Bart is making snacks and uses 5 raisins for each snack. About how many snacks can Bart make with a small box of raisins? Explain how you found your answer.

   _____

   _____

   _____

   _____

Name_____

Multiplication and Arrays

Evelyn likes to take gifts to people who are in the hospital.
She knows there are 6 floors at the hospital that are for
patients. On each floor there are 4 nurses' stations,
and each nurses' station is in charge of 12 patient rooms.
You may draw a picture to help for 1–6.

1. How many patient rooms are there on each floor?

_____

2. How many patient rooms are there altogether?

_____

3. Two of the floors only allow one patient in each room.
   These are called private rooms. How many private rooms
   are there in the hospital?

_____

4. Four of the floors are set up to have two patients per room.
   These are called semiprivate rooms. How many
   semiprivate rooms are there in the hospital?

_____

5. If each of the semiprivate rooms is full, how many patients
   are in the semiprivate rooms?

_____

6. **Writing in Math** How many tens would there be in an
   array for 3×22? Explain.

_____

_____

_____

Name_____

Breaking Numbers Apart to Multiply

Lemonade A store sells lemonade in 5 different-sized cups.

Size	Ounces
Monster	72
Extra large	65
Large	34
Medium	21
Regular	16

1. Every day Lonnie buys a medium lemonade. How many ounces of lemonade does he purchase in 5 days?

   _____

2. Bob bought 3 monster lemonades for his friends. How many ounces of lemonade did he buy altogether?

   _____

3. Which is larger, 4 large lemonades or 6 medium lemonades?

   _____

4. Which is larger, 8 regular lemonades or 2 extra large lemonades?

   _____

5. **Writing in Math** Tom said you do not need to break apart any numbers to find 3×30. Is he correct? Explain.

   _____

   _____

   _____

   _____

Multiplying Two-Digit Numbers

For 1–5, find the total number of things that are
in the containers.

1. A carton of eggs contains 12 eggs. How many eggs are
   there in 5 cartons?

   _____

2. Lori bought 6 bags with 21 ladybug pins in each bag. How
   many ladybug pins are there in all?

   _____

3. A bottle of perfume contains 19 oz of perfume. There
   are 8 bottles of perfume in a box. How many ounces of
   perfume does a full box contain?

   _____

4. The cafeteria ordered 6 crates of chocolate milk and
   2 crates of regular milk. Each crate contains 27 cartons of
   milk. How many cartons of milk were ordered altogether?

   _____

5. Joe bought 7 packs of baseball cards that had 22 cards in
   each pack. How many cards in all did he buy?

   _____

6. **Writing in Math** Marcus delivers 47 newspapers every day
   from Monday through Saturday. On Sunday, he delivers
   three times that many. Explain how to find the number of
   papers that Marcus delivers on Sunday.

   _____

   _____

Multiplying Three-Digit Numbers

Name_____

The table shows the distances between four major cities.

	Chicago, IL	Detroit, MI	New York City, NY	Pittsburgh, PA
Chicago, IL	0	308	787	460
Detroit, MI	308	0	614	286
New York, NY	787	614	0	370
Pittsburgh, PA	460	286	370	0

1. Joann and her family drove from Pittsburgh to New York City and then back again. How many miles did they drive?

   _____

2. If a businessperson drives from Detroit to Chicago and back 3 times for a total of 6 one-way trips between the cities, how many miles did the person drive in all?

   _____

3. If a businessperson makes 4 trips from New York to Detroit and back for a total of 8 one-way trips between the cities, how many miles did the person drive in all?

   _____

4. Which is farther, 7 times the distance between New York City and Pittsburgh or 4 times the distance between New York City and Detroit?

   _____

   _____

5. **Writing in Math** To multiply 4×302, how many times do you have to regroup? Explain.

   _____

   _____

Multiplying Money

Jill is shopping for school supplies. The chart shows the prices of some items.

Pens	$0.99 each
Folders	$1.49 each
Paper	$2.79 each
Binders	$3.99 each

1. How much would 4 pens cost?

_____

2. How much would 6 folders cost?

_____

3. How much would 3 packs of paper cost?

_____

4. How much would 5 binders cost?

_____

5. How much would 2 binders and 2 folders cost?

_____

6. Writing in Math Jill has $20.00 to spend. Can she buy 3 folders, 3 packs of paper, and 2 binders with the money? Explain.

_____

_____

_____

_____

Name_____

Choose a Computation Method

Steller's sea lions live in the north Pacific Ocean. The chart below lists some facts about Steller's sea lions.

Steller's Sea Lion Facts

	Average Weight	Average Length
Sea lion pup	23 kg	112 cm
Adult male sea lion	566 kg	282 cm
Adult female sea lion	263 kg	228 cm

1. If a female sea lion gives birth to 2 average-sized pups, about how much is their combined weight? Tell what computation method you used.

_____

2. About how much would a group of 8 adult male sea lions weigh? Tell what computation method you used.

_____

3. If 5 female sea lions lay down head to tail, about what would their total length be? Tell what computation method you used.

_____

4. About how much would 10 adult males weigh? Tell what computation method you used.

_____

5. **Writing in Math** Miles said that paper and pencil is the best method to find 13×3. Do you agree? Explain.

_____

_____

_____

Name_____

Use Logical Reasoning

Street Smart On Megan's block, the first house number on her side of the street is 501. The next house on her side of the street is 503, and the one next to that is 505. The last house is 517. How many houses are there on Megan's side of the street?

Read and Understand

1. What do you know?

_____

_____

2. What are you trying to find?

_____

_____

Plan and Solve

3. What strategy will you use?

_____

_____

4. Solve the problem. Write the answer in a complete sentence.

_____

_____

Look Back and Check

5. Is your answer reasonable?

_____

_____

Using Objects to Divide

Home computers can print out address labels in many sizes for addressing packages and letters. You may draw pictures to help.

1. A sheet of address labels has 42 labels. There are 3 columns of labels. How many labels are in each column?

    _____

2. A different sheet of address labels has 96 labels. There are 4 columns of labels. How many labels are in each column?

    _____

3. John has $0.70 in nickels. How many nickels does John have?

    _____

4. A serving of low-fat salad dressing contains 8 g of fat. There are 96 g of fat in a bottle. How many servings of salad dressing are in the bottle?

    _____

5. A bottle of apple juice has 56 oz of apple juice in it. There are 2 oz samples of the juice being served in the juice aisle. How many samples can the server get from one bottle of apple juice?

    _____

6. **Writing in Math** Yvette said that you do not have to regroup leftover tens when using objects to divide 69 ÷ 3. Is she correct? Explain.

    _____

    _____

    _____

Breaking Numbers Apart to Divide   PS 11-13

Volcano Models The fourth-grade students are studying volcanoes. For each student to make a model of a volcano, they need 84 c of salt, 69 c of flour, 2 gal of water, 24 boxes of baking soda, and 2 bottles of vinegar.

1. Four students have volunteered to bring in salt. How much salt should each student bring?

   _____

2. Three students have volunteered to bring in flour. How much flour should each student bring?

   _____

3. There are 3 fourth-grade teachers. They have each decided to bring in 15 c of flour. How much flour will each of the 3 student volunteers need to bring in now?

   _____

4. Two students are bringing the baking soda. How many boxes should each student bring?

   _____

5. A container of salt has about 2 c of salt in it. How many 2 c containers of salt are needed?

   _____

6. **Writing in Math** Can you use the break apart method to find $95 \div 5$? Explain.

   _____

   _____

   _____

Dividing

Mrs. Sorenson has 26 copies of her third-grade social studies textbook. She keeps them on shelves near the back of her classroom. Each shelf holds 8 textbooks.

1. How many shelves can Mrs. Sorenson completely fill with textbooks?

_____

2. How many shelves will have at least 1 textbook on them?

_____

3. How many textbooks will be on the shelf that is not completely filled?

_____

Jacob is buying storage boxes to store all of the things he does not use very often. He sees that the boxes are on sale for $5 each including tax. Jacob has $83 that he can spend on the boxes.

4. How many storage boxes can Jacob purchase?

_____

5. How much money will Jacob have left after he has purchased as many storage boxes as he can?

_____

6. Writing in Math Explain how you found your answer to Exercise 5.

_____

_____

_____

Name_____

Interpreting Remainders

Garden Vince is constructing a wall of rocks around his garden.
He needs 73 rocks and can carry 3 rocks at a time. How many
trips will it take Vince to carry 73 rocks to his garden?

(Read and Understand)

1. How many rocks does Vince need? How many rocks can
   he carry at a time?

   _____

2. What are you trying to find?

   _____

   _____

(Plan and Solve)

3. What equation do you need to solve?

   _____

4. What does the remainder represent in the answer?

   _____

   _____

5. Solve the problem. Write the answer in a complete sentence.

   _____

(Look Back and Check)

6. Is your answer reasonable?

   _____

   _____

PROBLEM-SOLVING APPLICATION

Take a Seat

At a baseball tournament, one team has 31 players and 2 coaches. A total of 6 people can sit on a bench. Will 5 benches be enough to seat everyone on the team?

Read and Understand

1. What do you know?

_____

_____

2. What are you trying to find?

_____

Plan and Solve

3. What is the first computation you must perform?

_____

4. What division equation do you need to solve?

_____

5. Solve the problem. Write the answer in a complete sentence.

_____

_____

Look Back and Check

6. Is your answer reasonable?

_____

_____

Customary Units of Capacity

Punch There are 16 students in Mr. Kelley's class. Each student drinks 1 c of punch.

1. How many quarts of punch will Mr. Kelley need for the class?

   _____

2. Will 1 gal of punch be enough to serve the 16 students?

   _____

3. If half the class drinks 2 c of punch and the other half of the class drinks 1 c, how many quarts of punch will Mr. Kelley need?

   _____

Humidifier Mr. Janis refills his humidifier with 2 qt of water every day.

4. How many cups of water does Mr. Janis put into the humidifier each day?

   _____

5. How many gallons of water does Mr. Janis put in the humidifier over 4 days?

   _____

6. How many pints of water does he use in 3 days?

   _____

7. **Writing in Math** Explain how you found the answer to Exercise 6.

   _____

   _____

   _____

   _____

   _____

Milliliters and Liters

Bird Care Carrie has a pet bird. She also enjoys taking care of the birds that visit her backyard.

1. Carrie gives her pet bird fresh water each day. Do you think she gives the bird more than or less than 1 L of water?

_____

2. Carrie refills the birdbath each week with fresh water. Do you think the birdbath holds 4 L or 4 mL of water?

_____

3. Every other week, Carrie scrubs the birdbath with soap and water. Do you think the bucket of water holds 8 mL or 8 L of water?

_____

Water Alan has 3 containers filled with water. Each container holds 250 mL of water.

4. Will all of the water fit in a 1 L container?

_____

5. If Alan has 2 L of water, how many 250 mL containers can he fill?

_____

6. If Alan has 2 L of water and then drank two 250 mL containers of water, how many milliliters of water does he have left?

_____

7. **Writing in Math** Walter said that 500 mL is the same as 5 L. Is he correct? Explain.

_____

_____

_____

PROBLEM-SOLVING STRATEGY
Work Backward

Note Cards Marsha had some note cards. She gave 21 note cards to her mother and 15 to her teacher. She then had 31 note cards left. How many note cards did Marsha begin with?

> **Read and Understand**

1. How many note cards did Marsha give to her mother? To her teacher?

_____

2. How many note cards did Marsha have left?

_____

3. What are you trying to find?

_____

_____

> **Plan and Solve**

4. What strategy will you use?

_____

5. Solve the problem. Write the answer in a complete sentence.

_____

_____

> **Look Back and Check**

6. Is your answer reasonable?

_____

Customary Units of Weight

Butter One stick of butter weighs 4 oz.

1. How many sticks are in 1 lb?

   _____

2. If a recipe called for $\frac{1}{2}$ lb of butter, how many sticks would you need?

   _____

3. One box of butter contains 4 sticks. Jan bought 3 boxes of butter. How much did they weigh in ounces? How much did they weigh in pounds?

   _____

Apples At the grocery store, Alice bought a bag of apples weighing 11 oz, Karen bought a bag weighing 1 lb 4 oz, and Mike bought a bag weighing 1 lb 13 oz.

4. How much more did Karen's bag weigh than Alice's?

   _____

5. How much more did Mike's bag weigh than Alice's?

   _____

6. What did Mike's and Karen's bags weigh altogether?

   _____

7. **Writing in Math** Explain how you found your answer to Exercise 6.

   _____

   _____

   _____

Grams and Kilograms

Traveling with a Cat Nancy is shopping for a cat carrier to take her pet on a plane trip. The cat weighs 4 kg.

1. The first carrier can hold a cat that weighs up to 2,500 g. Will this be enough to hold Nancy's cat?

   _____

2. The next carrier can hold a cat that weighs up to 3,000 g. Will this be enough to hold Nancy's cat?

   _____

3. How many grams will the carrier have to hold for it to be large enough for Nancy's cat?

   _____

Cherries Pam needs to buy some cherries for pies she is going to bake.

4. One bag of cherries weighs 1,100 g and another weighs 1 kg. Which bag is heavier?

   _____

5. Another bag weighs 1,700 g. Is that more than or less than 2 kg?

   _____

6. Pam buys two bags of cherries, one weighing 1,350 g and another weighing 1,650 g. How much is that in kilograms?

   _____

7. **Writing in Math** Bart said that his calculator probably weighs about 300 g. Does that seem reasonable? Explain.

   _____

   _____

Temperature

Highs and Lows Justin charted the high and low temperatures for a week. Use the chart for 1–5.

	Mon	Tues	Wed	Thur	Fri	Sat	Sun
High	60°F	58°F	50°F	41°F	51°F	36°F	30°F
Low	40°F	39°F	35°F	28°F	35°F	21°F	18°F

1. What was the difference between the high and low temperatures on Monday?

_____

2. On which two days of the week was there exactly a 15°F difference between the high and low temperatures?

_____

3. On Tuesday, about how high was the temperature in °C?

_____

4. On Thursday, about how high was the temperature in °C?

_____

5. **Writing in Math** On Sunday, was it cold enough for water to freeze? Explain.

_____

_____

_____

_____

_____

Describing Chances

Marbles Greg and Tom are going to play marbles. They have the 10 marbles shown to choose from. Describe each event as likely, unlikely, certain, or impossible.

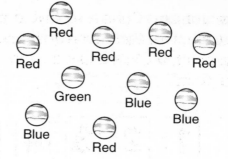

Red
Red   Red   Red   Red
Green   Blue
Blue   Blue
Red

1. Choosing a marble

_____

2. Choosing a red marble

_____

3. Choosing a green marble

_____

4. Choosing a black marble

_____

5. Paula's father bought her a balloon. Paula picked it from a bundle that included 7 red-and-white-striped balloons, 2 blue balloons, and 2 yellow balloons. Is choosing a blue or yellow balloon likely, unlikely, certain, or impossible?

_____

6. **Writing in Math** What would you have to change about the balloon bundle to make it certain that Paula would choose a blue balloon?

_____

_____

_____

Fair and Unfair

Cards Joe and Chris are playing a game. They are using the 5 cards shown. Each time Joe picks an odd-numbered card, he gets a point. If Chris picks an even-numbered card, then he gets a point.

 1 2 3 4 5

1. What is the chance of a player drawing an odd-numbered card?

   _____

2. What is the chance of a player drawing an even-numbered card?

   _____

3. Is this game fair? If not, who has the best chance of winning?

   _____

4. Joe and Chris make a new game using colored cards. When Joe picks a green card he gets a point, and when Chris picks a blue card he gets a point. If Joe and Chris have 10 cards and 2 of them are yellow, how many green cards and blue cards do they need for the game to be fair?

   _____

5. **Writing in Math** What could Joe and Chris do to make their numbered card game fair?

   _____

   _____

   _____

   _____

Probability

Take a Spin Kim and Karen are using a spinner to divide a bag of buttons. Each player spins and gets to take that number of buttons from the bag.

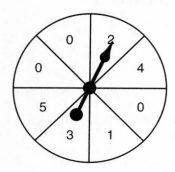

What is the probability of

1. choosing 0 buttons? _____

2. choosing an even number of buttons? _____

3. choosing 5 buttons? _____

4. choosing an odd number of buttons? _____

5. choosing less than 2 buttons? _____

6. choosing at least 1 button? _____

7. choosing 1 or 2 buttons? _____

8. **Writing in Math** On the spinner, are the chances of spinning any of the numbers from 1 to 5 equally likely? Explain.

_____

_____

_____

PROBLEM-SOLVING SKILL
Writing to Explain

Number Cube Carly tossed a number cube five times and got the numbers 2, 6, 4, 6, and 2. Predict whether it was more likely that Carly was using a cube numbered 1, 2, 3, 4, 5, and 6 or a cube numbered 2, 2, 4, 4, 6, and 6.

Read and Understand

1. How many times did Carly toss the number cube? _____

2. What were the results? _____

3. What are you trying to find?

_____

_____

Plan and Solve

4. How can you solve the problem? Explain.

_____

_____

5. Write your answer in a complete sentence.

_____

_____

Look Back and Check

6. Is your answer reasonable?

_____

_____

_____

Name_____

At the Movies

Jim went to a movie on a Saturday afternoon. He spent $7.00 on a ticket and $2.50 on popcorn. Then he found a $5.00 bill on the floor of the theater. After the movie, he bought a drink for $1.50. He then had $7.50 left. How much money did Jim have before he went to the movie?

Read and Understand

1. How much money did Jim spend? How much did he find?

_____

2. How much did he have left?   _____

3. What are you trying to find?

_____

_____

Plan and Solve

4. What strategy will you use to solve this problem?

_____

5. Solve the problem. Write the answer in a complete sentence.

_____

_____

Look Back and Check

6. Is your work reasonable?

_____

_____